International
Restaurant English

International
Restaurant English

Leila Keane

ENGLISH LANGUAGE TEACHING

Prentice Hall

New York London Toronto Sydney Tokyo

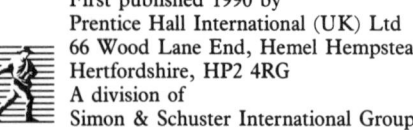

First published 1990 by
Prentice Hall International (UK) Ltd
66 Wood Lane End, Hemel Hempstead
Hertfordshire, HP2 4RG
A division of
Simon & Schuster International Group

Typeset in 11/13pt Plantin by
MHL Typesetting Ltd, Coventry
Printed and bound in Great Britain at the
University Press, Cambridge.

Library of Congress Cataloging-in-Publication Data

Keane, L.L. (Leila L.)
    International restaurant English / Leila Keane.
        p. cm. − (English language teaching)
        ISBN 0-13-473505-6 : $9.95
        1. English language − Conversation and phrase books
(for restaurant and hotel personnel). 2. English language −
Textbooks for foreign speakers. 3. Restaurant management
− Terminology.   I. Title.   II. Series.
PE1116.R47K44   1990   89-39457
428.3'4'024642—dc20   CIP

British Library Cataloguing in Publication Data

Keane, Leila
    International restaurant English. − (English language
teaching series)
    I. Title   II. Series
    428.6

    ISBN 0-13-473505-6

---

1 2 3 4 5   93 92 91 90 89

Contents

Introduction

Who is the course for?
- Students in, for example, catering colleges who are attending English language classes.
- Much of the work is also suitable for personnel already working in restaurants, bars, etc. who wish to study English on their own.

What is the purpose of the course?
To prepare learners for typical situations in which they have to understand and respond in English to an international restaurant or bar clientèle.

What is the language level?
The course is for learners ranging from the elementary level — namely those who have studied some English or who have acquired some English in their work — to more advanced speakers, who need to study systematically the English of food and beverage service.

What does the course consist of?
- The course book, which comprises:
  15 teaching units
  The text of the tape-recorded exercises
  A table of unit contents
  A word list of ingredients and cooking methods in: English, French, Spanish, Italian and German.
- A cassette of recorded exercises. This is an essential part of the course.

What are the main features of the course?
- Learners practise *understanding* questions, requests, etc. in typical siutations, from customers who have different accents and express themselves in different ways.
- They practise *using* a more limited but adaptable range of *active language for speaking* to customers.

- There is also some *reading* and *writing* practice where it is relevant — for example, in the unit on banqueting arrangements.
- Each unit is based on a *topic* — an aspect of restaurant and bar work, such as taking orders or making reservations. The unit teaches items of vocabulary, 'functional' language and grammar that go with the topic.
- It is possible to study the units *in any order* — they are self-contained.
- It is also possible to *omit exercises* that are not relevant to a particular group of students, if they deal with *a point of language* that the students already know, or with *a topic* that they do not need.
- Some language elements (such as polite questions or expressions of quantity) occur *in more than one unit*, because such language is needed in different kinds of situations, and also because it is useful for students to encounter key language items more than once.
- In nearly all the language practice, students play the part of *members of staff who are dealing with customers*.
- Students have many opportunities to apply the language work to *local stiuations*, and to bring their *personal experience, knowledge and interests* into the work.
- Many of the exercises ask students to work in *pairs* or *small groups*, usually in realistic customer—staff situations.

How is each unit structured?
Each unit has four parts:

1 *To start you off*. This section:

- helps students to marshall *the facts they already know* about a topic
- may provide *new information* about the topic
- introduces *relevant language*

The work includes discussion, some reading and writing, labelling drawings, matching words and pictures, etc. Some of the discussion can be in the students' own language.

2 *Developing the topic*. This is the largest section. Students have *practice in understanding and using items of vocabulary, 'functional' language and grammar* that are associated with the topic of the unit. Various 'mini' exercises lead to slightly larger-scale work, in which the students are guided in speaking in longer transactions. An important part of the section is the taped work: this usually comprises two exercises, in which students have to understand what customers are saying, and practise saying the waiting staff's words.

3 *Follow-up*. This is a shorter section. In it, the students use the language they have learnt in the previous sections to deal with *whole situations* that are likely to occur in real life. They have an opportunity to bring in local situations and to include their own knowledge, experience and interests.

In some units, this section also includes some quick revision of *vocabulary*.

4 *Language reference*. This section *lists the main items* of vocabulary, grammar and 'functional' language in the unit. Students may need to refer to it while working through the unit; it is also a useful general resource, and a help in revision.

Methodology

The approach of the course is basically *communicative*: that is, in nearly all the work in the *Developing the topic* and *Follow-up* sections, students play the parts of food and beverage staff in realistic situations. The work ranges from closely structured grammar practice, to closely guided interaction chains, to relatively open-ended rôle-play.

The situations and settings

The main focus of the course is on the kinds of eating and drinking establishments that cater for *an international clientèle*, and on the language that is suitable in such establishments. There is also guidance on the language suitable in more *informal* settings, where this is markedly different.

Working without a teacher

A learner working alone can do most of the work in this book. For *vocabulary* work, a bilingual dictionary and a good up-to-date monolingual dictionary (such as the Longman Dictionary of Contemporary English) are recommended. For *discussions*, it will obviously be best if a partner can be found. The discussion can usually be in the learner's own language. For *pair work*, if there is no partner, the learner can record one participant's words on tape and respond to the tape. Alternatively, she or he can prepare and write out one participant's words on a series of pieces of paper, then pick up the pieces of paper, one at a time, and respond to them.

Acknowledgements

We are grateful to the following for their advice and help during the preparation of this book:

Donald Adamson, who laid its foundation in writing *International Hotel English* and then continued to help and advise.

Diana Bruno, of the Institut de Tourisme et d'hôtellerie du Québec.

Members of the School of Catering, Waltham Forest College for Further and Higher Education, London.

For permission to use their material:
Barnaby's Photo Library (page 1).
Holiday Inn Marble Arch and Manchester (page 1).
Zefa Picture Library (UK) Ltd (page 1).
School of Catering, Waltham Forest College for Further and Higher Education, London (pages 44 and 45).
Woodford Moat House Ltd, Woodford Green, Essex (page 109).
The May Fair Inter-Continental Hotel, London (pages 114 and 116).

Contents of units

Unit	Language functions and skills	Grammar	Vocabulary
1	Describing a restaurant. Explaining its amenities and services. Giving opening times. Greetings and goodbyes. Answers to questions. } Formal and informal	Present Simple: *We accept credit cards.* *can: You can dance.* Short answers: *Yes, there is,* etc. Compound nouns: *waitress service, a three-course meal.*	Types of restaurants. Names of meals. Types of menus. Amenities and services.
2	Explaining the purpose of equipment. Understanding complaints about equipment. Apologizing. Offering to do things.	*for* + gerund: *That knife's for cutting cheese.* Countable and uncountable nouns: *a jug of water, some water; another knife, some other knives.* *I'll* for offers: *I'll bring you another knife.*	Names of cutlery, chinaware, etc. Describing defects (for comprehension).
3	Giving and understanding spellings. Taking down reservations. Questions about reservations. Confirming reservations.	*would* in polite questions: *Would that be for lunch?* *could* in polite requests: *Could you spell that, please?*	Two spelling alphabets: *A as in Alpha,* etc.; *A for Andrew,* etc. Words and expressions relating to reservations.
4	Understanding requests for (a) special arrangements, (b) changes to reservations. Meeting requests. Not meeting requests. Suggesting alternatives.	*could* in suggestions: *You could have a table at seven.*	Special diets. Special positions in a restaurant. Premises and furniture. Words and expressions relating to changes in reservations. Expressions of agreement, regret, etc.

Unit	Language functions and skills	Grammar	Vocabulary
5	Describing the position of a restaurant. Explaining how to get to a restaurant.	Prepositions describing position. Prepositions describing direction. Ordinal numbers: *first, second*, etc.	Landmarks. Streets and roads. Verbs used in giving directions.
6	Receiving and placing customers. Asking about customers' wishes. Polite responses to customers' requests. Taking orders for starters and main courses. Making recommendations. Describing wines.	*would* when asking about wishes: *Would you like an aperitif? can* and *would* when recommending: *I can recommend the salmon. I would suggest the St Emilion.* Countable and uncountable nouns: *a roll, some rolls, some water.* Comparisons: *Wine A is lighter than Wine B. Wine B is more full-bodied/not as light as Wine A.*	Sections of a menu. Dishes in a menu. Words describing wines.
7	Explaining the composition of starters and main courses. Explaining their preparation.	Compound nouns: *rice stuffing.* Part participle: *sliced mushrooms.* Passive: *The tomatoes are stuffed with rice.* Countable and uncountable nouns. Expressions of quantity: *no, very little/ very few, a lot of*, etc.	Ingredients in starters and main courses. Adjectives describing ingredients and dishes. Verbs relating to preparation and cooking. Expressions for describing dishes.
8	Understanding customers' opinions and wishes. Asking about customers' wishes. Meeting customers' requests. Not meeting customers' requests. Suggesting alternatives.	*I'll* for offers: *I'll bring you one.* Expressions of quantity (for comprehension): *just a little, plenty*, etc.	Adjectives for praising or criticizing food (for comprehension). Names of accompaniments. Phrases for responding to customers' requests.

Unit	Language functions and skills	Grammar	Vocabulary
9	Explaining the composition and preparation of desserts. Describing and comparing desserts. Describing and comparing cheeses. Describing different kinds of coffee. Taking orders for the later stages of a meal. Making recommendations.	Past participle: *chopped nuts.* Comparisons: *The Gorgonzola is stronger than the Brie. The cake contains more sugar than the fruit salad. The fruit salad is less rich and contains less sugar than the cake.*	Ingredients in desserts. Adjectives describing desserts. Adjectives describing cheeses. Verbs relating to the preparation of desserts.
10	Taking orders for drinks. Asking about customers' wishes. Making suggestions.	*can* and *would* in questions: *What can I get you? Would you like some ice? How about?* for suggestions: *How about a sherry?*	Alcoholic and non-alcoholic drinks. Adjectives describing drinks. Expressions of quantity (for comprehension).
11	Explaining bills. Asking how customers want to pay. Meeting or not meeting customers' wishes about paying.	Passive: *Service is included. will be* for polite questions: *How will you be paying? could* for polite requests: *Could you sign here, please?*	Figures and calculations. Items on a bill. Methods of payment.
12	Apologizing. Asking about problems. Maintaining customers' confidence. Offers of action. Explaining regulations. Polite refusals. Suggesting other courses of action.	*I'll* in offers of action: *I'll change it for you immediately. have to* and *may not* when stating regulations: *Gentlemen have to wear jackets. Ladies may not wear casual trousers.*	Various phrases for performing the functions listed.
13	Stating the dimensions of a room. Describing a room. Explaining banqueting and conference charges. Asking about customers' wishes and intentions. Making suggestions. Writing a semi-formal letter.	Passive: *It is carpeted. would* for explanations: *That would include wines. How about?* for suggestions: *How about a band?*	Types of banqueting events. Amenities and services for banquets. Equipment for conferences. Various phrases for the language functions listed.

Unit	Language functions and skills	Grammar	Vocabulary
14	Taking orders for breakfast. Asking about customers' wishes.	*would* in various polite questions.	Items in a breakfast menu. Methods of cooking eggs.
15	Writing a curriculum vitae. Writing a letter of application. Attending a job interview. Stating one's attitude towards a possible job.	Simple past for past experience: *At the Ritz I worked* ... Present continuous for current activities: *I am learning to* ... Present simple for regular duties: *I often work* ... *would* for attitudes towards a possible job: *I would enjoy that.*	Words in job advertisements and curricula vitae. Expressions in a letter of application. Adverbs of frequency.

Restaurants and their services

To start you off

1 These are five different sorts of places where people can eat and drink. Can you find the right description for each one? For example: *picture 1 – luxury restaurant*

bar – coffee shop – informal restaurant serving national or regional dishes – luxury restaurant – night club

2   Members of staff are on the telephone, explaining the services at the five establishments. Decide which sentences apply to which establishment. For example: *luxury restaurant: (d), (j).*

(Some sentences may apply to more than one establishment.)

(a) We serve typical local dishes.
(b) You can dance to our band.
(c) You can have a snack with your drinks.
(d) Dinner is à la carte, Sir.
(e) We have an excellent floor show.
(f) We have two sorts of dinner menu: à la carte and a three-course, fixed price menu.
(g) You can have a quick snack here any time.
(h) We make all the pasta ourselves.
(i) You can gamble if you like.
(j) We are noted for our haute cuisine, Madam.
(k) We serve sandwiches, salads, cakes and beverages.

3   Can you name eating and drinking establishments of the five kinds in your area? For example: *The Ritz is a luxury restaurant.*

Are there eating and drinking establishments in your area which do not fit any of the descriptions in Exercises 1 and 2? What are they? How are they different?

For example: *The Cafe Grande is like a coffee shop, but*

it serves . . ./doesn't serve . . .
it has . . ./doesn't have . . .
the customer can . . ./can't . . .

4   Imagine you are writing advertisements for the five establishments on page 1. Which of these phrases would you use for which establishment? For example: *luxury restaurant = elegant surroundings, sophisticated atmosphere . . .*

elegant surroundings – cosy atmosphere – friendly atmosphere – relaxed atmosphere – live music, of course! – reasonably priced meals – authentic national dishes – international cabaret – superb cuisine – sophisticated atmosphere – sophisticated entertainment – traditional dishes – our very lively trio – quick service – impeccable service – delicious, home-made dishes – excellent wine cellar – dinner and dancing – business lunches – romantic dinners

Developing the topic

5 Below are different ways of saying the time. Write down the times in figures.
For example: *(a) = 1500 hours.*

(a) three p.m.
(b) three a.m.
(c) half past three in the morning
(d) a quarter to three in the afternoon
(e) a quarter past eight in the evening
(f) ten o'clock at night
(g) noon/midday
(h) midnight

6 You will hear members of staff from four of the establishments on page 1.
They are answering telephone enquiries about opening times. Listen, and put ticks
(√) to show the days when they are open, and crosses (×) to show when they are
closed. Then listen again and note down the opening hours.

	Times	**Mon**	**Tue**	**Wed**	**Thur**	**Fri**	**Sat**	**Sun**
1. Luxury restaurant Lunch Dinner	*12.30* – .... – *24.00*	☑ ☐	☑ 	☑ 	☑ 	☑ 	☒ 	☑
2. Bar	..... –	☐	☐	☐	☐	☐	☐	☐
3. Informal restaurant Lunch Dinner	..... – .... –	☐ ☐	☐ ☐	☐ ☐	☐ ☐	☐ ☐	☐ ☐	☐ ☐
4. Coffee shop	..... –	☐	☐	☐	☐	☐	☐	☐

7 |OO|

(a) Check your answers to Exercise 6 with the tapescript on page 130.

(b) Play the tape again, while you follow the words in the tapescript.

(c) Close your book, and play the tape again, stopping it at suitable points, so that you can repeat the waiter's/waitress's words. For example: *Yes, Sir.* (Pause, repeat.) *We're open for lunch every day except Saturdays,* (pause, repeat,) *and for dinner every day.* (Pause, repeat.)

(d) For further practice, play the tape again, with your book open. This time, do not stop the tape but say the waiter's/waitress's words with them, at the same time and at the same speed. Speak quietly — just loudly enough to hear yourself.

8 There are differences in the staff's language at the formal and informal establishments. Write down the missing equivalents.

Formal	Informal
Good morning/afternoon/... ...., Sir/Madam. Not at all, Sir/Madam. ... .../...	*Hello!* Thanks! ...'s ... ...! Bye!

9

			Times		Days
We're open We're closed	for	lunch dinner	from one to/till three (o'clock)		on Mondays to Saturdays. every day (of the week).
We open We close			at	one (o'clock) midnight	every day except Mondays. on Mondays.

Use this table to practise describing the opening hours of restaurants. For example:

We're open for lunch from one to three on Mondays to Saturdays.
We're closed for lunch on Sundays.

10 Work with a partner. Take turns to be A (a waiter/waitress in an eating or drinking establishment) or B (a customer). Student A should think of the opening days and times of four formal or four informal establishments. (They can be places you know, or you can invent them.) Student B should telephone Student A for the information. Use the language from Exercises 8 and 9.

11 A **club** where people go at **night** = a night club. Join the words below in the same way.

(a) A **card** which allows a person **credit** = a *credit* _____ _____
(b) A **dinner** which has a **set menu** = a *set –* _____ _____ *dinner*
(c) A **glass** for **wine** = a _____ _____
(d) A **bowl** for **soup** = a _____ _____
(e) **Service** by **waitresses** = waitresses service = waitress service
(f) A **lunch** of **three courses** = a _____ _____ _____
(g) A **restaurant** with **four stars** = a _____ _____ _____
(h) A **menu** with **fixed prices** = a _____ _____ _____
(i) A **cellar** where **wines** are stored = _____ _____
(j) A **list** of **wines** available = a _____ _____
(k) A **chair** with **wheels** = a _____ _____

12 Study the notice. Then cover the words, but do not cover the symbols. You are giving information about restaurants. Complete the sentences.

Symbol	Meaning
★★★★★	Very luxurious, with excellent cuisine (a five-star restaurant)
★★★	Excellent cuisine
alc £20–30 L	A typical three-course à la carte lunch costs £20 to £30
set £25 D	A three-course set menu (table d'hôte) dinner costs £25
(car symbol)	There is parking
(no-smoking symbol)	There is a no-smoking section in the restaurant
(musician symbol)	There is live music (live = not recorded; played by musicians)
(tree symbol)	You can eat out of doors (in a graden/on a terrace/by a swimming pool/...)
(binoculars symbol)	There is a beautiful view
(quiet symbol)	The restaurant is in a quiet area
(swimming symbol)	There is swimming (in a pool/in the sea/...)
Res	Reservations are advisable
Res +	Reservations are necessary
CrC: A.Ex, Eur, Vi, DC	The restaurant accepts: American Express, Eurocard, Visa and Diners Club credit cards

(a) We're a very l-x-r---- restaurant, Sir, with ex-----nt c--s-n-.
(b) Our c--s-n- is very good, Madam. We're a thr-- st-- restaurant.
(c) The cost of a three c--r--l-n-- is £20 to £30.
(d) The cost of our three c--r-- s-t m--- for d----r is £25.
(e) There's indoor p--k---.
(f) There's a no-sm-----s------ in the restaurant.
(g) There's l--- m---- in the evenings.
(h) You can eat o-- of d----.
(i) There's a beautiful v--- from the restaurant.
(j) We're in a very qu--- a---.
(k) You can sw-- in our p--l.
(l) Reserv------ are ad-------.
(m) Reserv------ are ne------y.
(n) We acc--- American Express cr---- c---s.

13   You will hear restaurant staff answering questions on the telephone from nine customers. Put a tick (√) to indicate what each customer is asking about. Write the name of the credit card if the customer asks about that.

						Res	CrC
1.							√ *Eurocard*
2.							
3.							
4.							
5.							
6.							
7.							
8.							
9.							

14   Study and then practise the staff's answers. Follow the procedure for Exercise 7 on page 4.

15   It is only in formal establishments that the staff say *Sir* or *Madam*. However, even in informal establishments, when staff answer questions it is not polite to say just *Yes* and *No*. It is usual to use 'short answers'.

Question	Short answer
Are you open on Mondays?	Yes, **we are.**/No, **we aren't.**
Do you serve alcohol?	Yes, **we do.**/No, ...
Is there any music?	Yes, ... **is.**/No, ...
Do you have a floorshow?	Yes, .../No, ...
Does your restaurant serve lunch?	Yes, **it** .../No, ...

Now practise asking and answering questions like this, in pairs.

Follow-up

16 Take turns to be A (a customer) and B (a waiter/waitress). Cover the words in Exercise 12. A should point at some of the symbols and B should explain them, like this:

A: *What does this mean?*
B: *It means that there is live music, Sir/Madam.*

17 Work with a partner. Student A reads the information below. Student B reads the information on page 151 in Appendix 2.

Student A

(a) You work in this formal restaurant.

> **The Pacific** **** alc £40–50 L £50–60 D
> Res+ CrC. A.Ex. Vi Open 12.30–3.00, 19.00–23.30

Student B, a tourist, rings you for information. Describe the restaurant, and answer his/her questions. Use words from Exercises 2, 6, 8, 9 and 12. Begin: 'The Pacific Restaurant. Good afternoon'.

(b) You are a tourist, phoning the Merida Restaurant (an informal restaurant) for information. You ask Student B, who works there, these questions:

Do you have a set menu for dinner?
How much is it?
Is there anywhere to park?
Do you have any live music?
Is it possible to eat outside?
Are you in a quiet area?
Do I need to book a table?
I suppose you accept Visa cards?

18 Work with one or two other students. Imagine that you are going to open a new restaurant. Use the notice in Exercise 12 as a check list for deciding:

— the kind of restaurant
— its opening times
— the kinds of menus and the prices
— its location
— its services and amenities (enjoyable features, for example a band, a beautiful view etc.)

Then write a small advertisement for it, giving this information and using some of the expressions from Exercise 4.

Language Reference

Types of restaurants etc.
a bar, a coffee house/shop, a night club, a luxury/formal/four-star restaurant, an informal restaurant, a snack bar, a fast-food restaurant.

Meals
Breakfast, brunch (= a combination of late breakfast and early lunch), lunch, afternoon tea, dinner; a meal, a snack; a course, a dish; a drink/beverage, an alcoholic drink/beverage.

Menus
an à la carte menu, a table d'hôte/fixed price/set price menu; a three-course lunch/dinner; haute cuisine, fine cuisine, nouvelle cuisine, traditional cuisine.

Amenities and services
surroundings, atmosphere, service; live music, a band, a floor show/cabaret, gambling; a non-smoking section, indoor and outdoor parking, a terrace, a beautiful view, a quiet area; a credit card, reservations.

Describing the setting, atmosphere and food
elegant, superb, sophisticated, impeccable, excellent; cosy, friendly, relaxed; reasonably priced; authentic, traditional; delicious.

Compound nouns
a night club, waitress service, a three-course meal.

Explaining amenities and services
You can dance.
There is a beautiful view.
We serve sandwiches.

We have a floor show.
We accept credit cards.
Reservations are advisable/necessary.

Polite expressions

Formal	*Informal*
Good morning (*until about 12.00*)	Hello!
Good afternoon (*12.30 until about 17.30*)	
Good evening (*after about 17.30*)	
Goodbye	Bye!/Bye bye!
Good night (= *goodbye after about 21.00*)	Good night
Thank you	Thanks
(In reply to *Thank you*): Not at all	That's all right!/You're welcome!

Answering questions

Formal	*Informal*
Yes, Sir/Madam/Certainly, Sir/Madam	Yes, you can/there is/we do/etc/
No, I'm (very) sorry, Sir/Madam	No, (I'm afraid) you can't/there isn't/we don't/etc.

Expressing regret
I'm (very) sorry; I'm afraid (= I regret to tell you).

Saying the time
01.00   one (o'clock) (in the morning) one a.m.*
11.30   eleven thirty (in the morning/a.m.) half past eleven (in the morning)
12.00   twelve (o'clock) noon/midday
14.00   two (o'clock) (in the afternoon) two p.m.**
15.15   three fifteen (in the afternoon/p.m.) a quarter past three (in the afternoon) (Am.E = a quarter after three).
19.45   seven forty-five (in the evening/p.m.) (a quarter to eight) (in the evening) (Am.E = a quarter of eight).
22.00   ten (o'clock) (at night); ten p.m.
24.00   twelve (o'clock); midnight
*   a.m. = ante meridiem (Latin) = before noon
** p.m. = post meridiem = after noon

On a restaurant table or tray

To start you off

1 Look at the pictures of a place setting for dinner and of a breakfast tray. Can you name the items? Check your answers on page 15.

Place setting for dinner

Tray setting for breakfast

2   Explain how to lay (a) a place setting for dinner and (b) a breakfast tray, using expressions like these:

First,	put	...	on ...
Then			in the middle
Next,			on the left
After that,			on the right

3   Here are some more items which may be on a restaurant table or a breakfast tray. Match the names with the pictures. For example: *(a) is a menu card.*

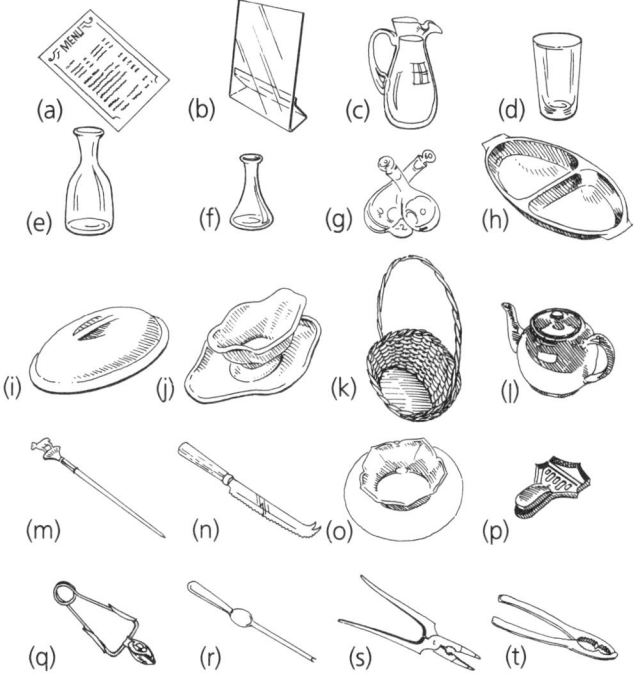

a fruit basket	a sauce boat	a tumbler
a cheese knife	a menu (card)	a (serving) dish
nut crackers (*plural*)	a menu holder	a lid
snail tongs (*plural*)	a tea pot	a lemon press
a water jug	a carafe	oil and vinegar (cruet)
a (flower) vase	a finger bowl	a lobster pick
		lobster crackers (*plural*)
		a skewer

4   Explain the function of items (n) to (t), using these words:

...	is are	for	breaking/cracking cutting extracting/getting out holding squeezing washing	...

For example: *A cheese knife is for cutting cheese.*
            Lobster crackers are for . . .

Developing the topic

5   First, listen to part A, in which six customers are asking questions. As you listen, decide whether each customer wants to know the *name* of an item or its *function*. Tick the right box.

	Name	Function			Name	Function
1.	✓	☐		4.	☐	☐
2.	☐	☐		5.	☐	☐
3.	☐	☐		6.	☐	☐

Now listen to part B, in which the waiting staff answer the customers' questions. Below are pictures of the items that the customers are asking about. Match the items and the customers. Use the table on the next page.

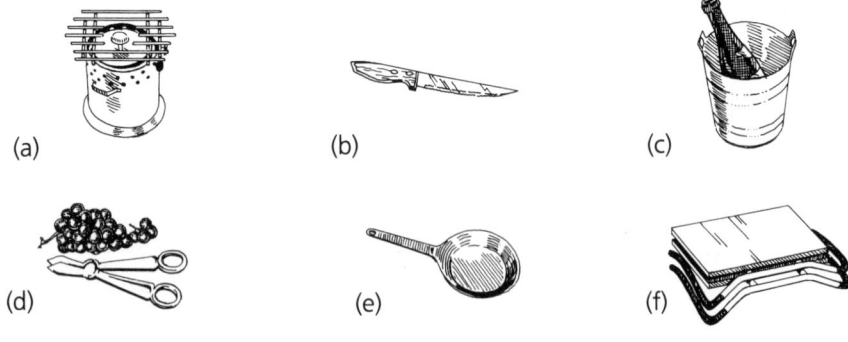

(a)   (b)   (c)

(d)   (e)   (f)

1. [c]   4. [ ]
2. [ ]   4. [ ]
3. [ ]   6. [ ]

Study and then practise the staff's answers. Follow the procedure for Exercise 7 on page 4.

6

A water jug = *a jug for holding water.*
A jug of water = *a jug which is full of water.*

Work with a partner. Take turns to be A or B.

Student A

I'd like some	some	water.
Could I have		coffee.
Could you bring me		tea.
Please bring us		wine.
		cream.
		jam.
		sugar.
		fruit.

Student B

Certainly, Sir/Madam. (Sure!/Yes, of course! *Informal.*)			
I'll bring you a	basket	of . . .	immediately.
	bowl		
	carafe		
	cup		
	dish		
	glass		
	jug		
	pot		

7 What could customers complain about here? Say what is wrong in each case, using the words in the box. In some cases, more than one word will fit.

> broken – cracked – chipped – dirty – stained – not clean – bent – blunt
> – empty – missing

For example: *The napkin is dirty/stained./The napkin isn't clean.*

8 Look at these examples:

I'd like *a/another* tumbler/jug of water. (*With 'countable' nouns, singular.*)
Could you bring us *some/some other* napkins/sugar tongs? (*With 'countable' nouns, plural.*)

Pictures 1–9 above show something that is wrong on nine different tables. Say what each table needs.

For example: *Table 1 needs another napkin/serviette.*

9 First, listen to part A, in which nine customers are complaining. Customers 1–5 are speaking to waiting staff at dinner; customers 6–9 are phoning a floor waiter at breakfast time. Note down briefly what is wrong in each case.

For example: *1. No ash tray / Ash tray missing*

Then listen to part B, in which the waiting staff apologize and offer to bring the items that are needed. Study and then practise the staff's answers. Follow the procedure for Exercise 7 on page 4.

Follow-up

10 Work with a partner. Take turns to be A or B. Student A covers the words in Exercises 1, 3 or 5, points to items in the pictures, and asks B, 'What's this?' B must answer as quickly as possible.
OR
Student A says the names of the items in the pictures, in mixed order. B must point to the items, as quickly as possible.

11 Work with a partner. Take turns to be A or B. Student A, the customer, should make a list of things which are wrong and complain to B, who is the waiter or waitress. B should apologize and offer to bring what is needed.

12 A guessing game. Work with a partner, and take turns to be A or B. A describes the function of a restaurant item; for example: *It's for cutting cheese.* B names the item; for example: *A cheese knife.*

Language reference

Flatware, cutlery, silverware, etc.
a side knife, a fish knife and fork, a table/joint/dinner knife and fork, a steak knife, a cheese knife, a soup spoon, a dessert spoon and fork, a coffee/tea spoon, a butter knife, a jam/preserve spoon, sugar tongs (*plural*), ice tongs (*plural*), nut crackers (*plural*), lobster crackers (*plural*), a lobster pick, snail tongs (*plural*), a skewer, a lemon press, a ladle

Hollow ware
a coffee/tea pot, a milk/cream jug, a sugar bowl, a (serving) dish and lid

China/Crockery
a (tea/coffee) cup, a saucer, a side/bread plate, a dinner plate, a soup plate/bowl, a butter dish, a jam/preserve dish, a sauce boat, a (flower) vase

Glassware
a (water) tumbler, a wine glass, a water jug, a carafe, a finger bowl

Other items
an ash tray, salt and pepper shakers (*plural*), an oil and vinegar cruet, a toast rack, a bread basket, a fruit basket, a tray, a tray cloth, a table cloth, a napkin/serviette,

an ice-bucket, grape-scissors (*plural*), a dish-warmer, a pan, a wine cooler, a bottle opener/corkscrew

Verbs
cut, crack, break, extract/get out, hold, squeeze, wash, cook, flambé (Am.E = flame), keep cool/hot

'Defect' adjectives (for comprehension)
dirty, not clean, stained, broken, chipped, cracked, bent, blunt, empty, missing

a water jug (= a jug for holding water) and **a jug of water** (= some water in a jug)

a/another and some/some other
I'll bring you *a* knife and *some other* plates.

Explaining functions (*for ...ing*)
That knife's *for cutting* cheese.

Apologizing
I'm very sorry, (Sir/Madam).

Offering to do something (*I'll = I will*)
I'll bring you a soup spoon immediately.

Reservations (1)
Basic exchanges

To start you off

1 Make a list of the kinds of information you need when you take down a table reservation over the telephone. For example: *1. For what day?*

2 Can you say the alphabet in English? Recite it together with other members of your class.

Developing the topic

3 Part A: You will hear someone spelling six names. Write them down.
Part B: Spell out the following names. After you have spelt each name, check the tape to see if you said the letters correctly. If necessary, repeat the spelling correctly.

1. Jay   2. King   3. Riel   4. How   5. Fox   6. McQueen

4 Work with a partner. Take turns to be A or B. Student A should spell out some names of people or places, including foreign names. B should write them down. You can continue, using one of the systems (Alpha-Bravo or Andrew-Benjamin) on page 24.

5 You will hear three people ringing the Deep Sea Restaurant to make reservations. Note down the information each person gives. Today is Wednesday.

	1.	2.	3.
Day:	*Wednesday*	. . . .	. . . .
Meal:	. . . .	. . . .	. . . .
Time:*	. . . .	. . . .	. . . .
Number of people:	. . . .	. . . .	. . . .
Name:	. . . .	. . . .	. . . .

*See Unit 1, Exercises 5 and 6 and the Language Reference section, for ways of saying the time.

6   Listen again, and write down the words each customer uses to give the following information:

She or he wants to reserve a table
1. *I'd like a table*
2. . . . .
3. . . . .

The day
1. . . . .
2. . . . .
3. *on Friday*

The number of people
1. . . . .
2. *for two*
3. . . . .

The meal
1. . . . .
2. *for tomorrow evening*
3. . . . .

The time
1. . . . .
2. *for about half past eight*
3. . . . .

Check your answers with the tapescript on page 135.

7   You will hear a telephone conversation between a waiter at the Deep Sea Restaurant and Mr Saarinen. First, listen and write down the waiter's actual words. The conversation is at natural speed and so you may need to listen more than once. Check your answers with the tapescript on pages 136−137.

Then listen again, and note down the information which Mr Saarinen gives.

Waiter   **Customer**

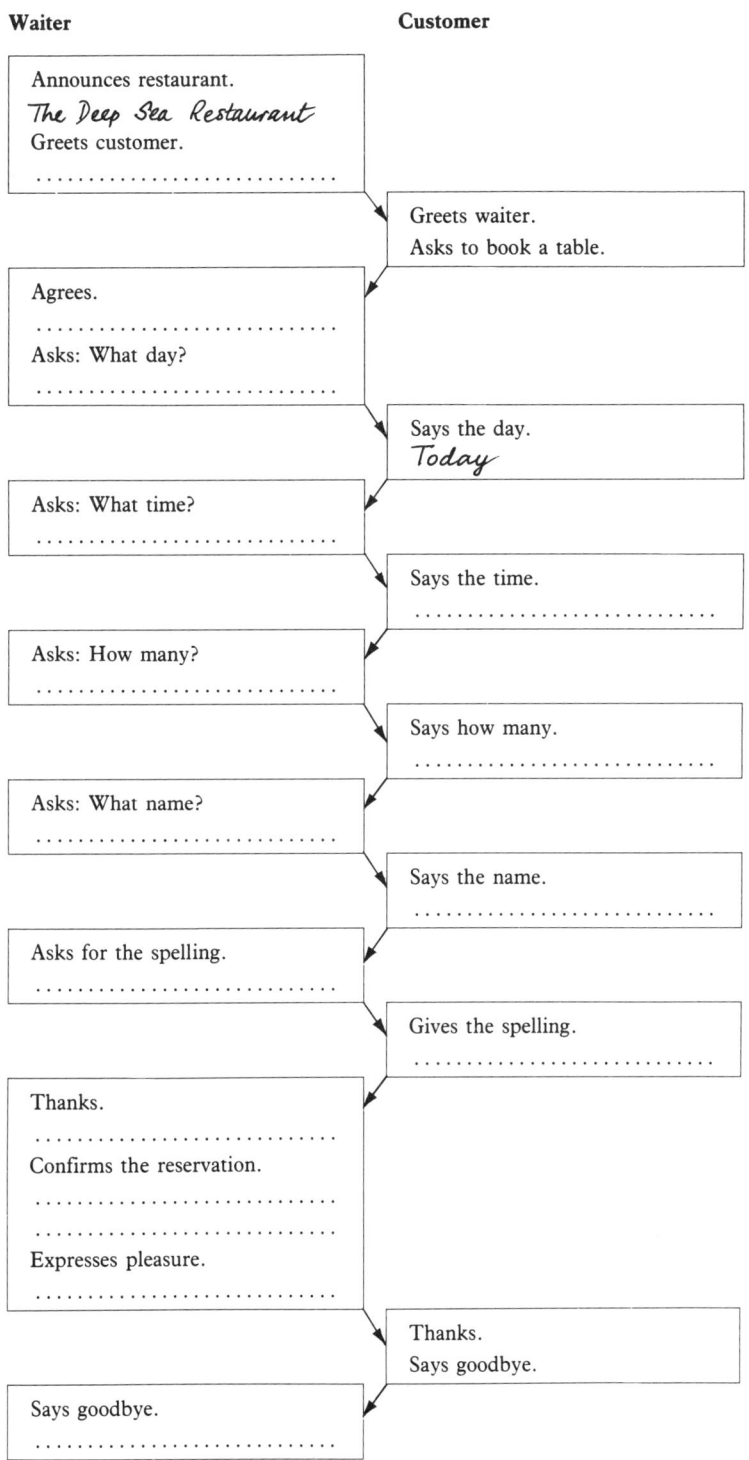

Announces restaurant.
The Deep Sea Restaurant
Greets customer.
....

Greets waiter.
Asks to book a table.

Agrees.
....
Asks: What day?
....

Says the day.
Today

Asks: What time?
....

Says the time.
....

Asks: How many?
....

Says how many.
....

Asks: What name?
....

Says the name.
....

Asks for the spelling.
....

Gives the spelling.
....

Thanks.
....
Confirms the reservation.
....
....
Expresses pleasure.
....

Thanks.
Says goodbye.

Says goodbye.
....

8 Play the tape again, and practise the waiter's words. Follow the procedure for Exercise 7 on page 4.

9 Notice how we use *would* in polite questions about a customer's *intentions* and *wishes* when making a reservation.

Intentions
For what day *would* that be?
How many people *would* there be in your party?

Wishes
Would you like a table near the band?

Complete the waiter's polite questions on the right.

Speech bubble (left)	Speech bubble (right)
For what day?	For what day *would that be ?*
For what time?	For what time _____ _____ _____?
Is that for lunch or dinner?	_____ _____ _____ for lunch or dinner?
For how many people?	For how many people _____ _____ _____?
How many people are there in your party?	How many people _____ there _____ in your party?

Now cover the words on the right, and practise asking the questions politely. Then practise with a partner or with the whole class. Cover the words on the right, and your partner or your teacher will ask the questions on the left, in any order: you should re-phrase each question politely.

10   Notice how we use *could* and *please* in polite *requests* to a customer: *Could you spell that, please?*

Complete the polite requests on the right, and then practise them. Work in the same way as in Exercise 9.

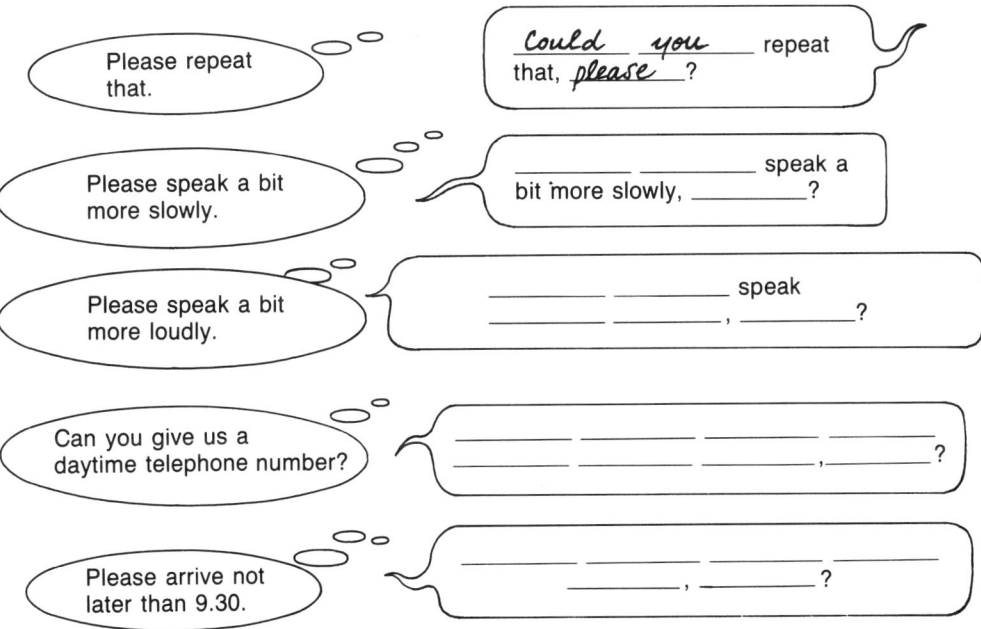

Follow-up

11 Work with a partner. Student A should read the information below. Student B should read the information on page 152.

(a) You are Mr De Vienne (in Exercise 7) and you are on the telephone to the Deep Sea Restaurant, where Student B is a waiter/waitress. Answer his/her questions.

(b) You work at the Deep Sea Restaurant. Student B, a customer, rings to make a reservation. Politely ask the following questions and make the requests. Note down the information.

What day?	Repeat that.
What time?	How do you spell it?
How may people?	Speak more slowly.
Name?	

(c) Continue working as in (a) and (b), but in (a) take the role of different customers, and be ready to answer B's questions.

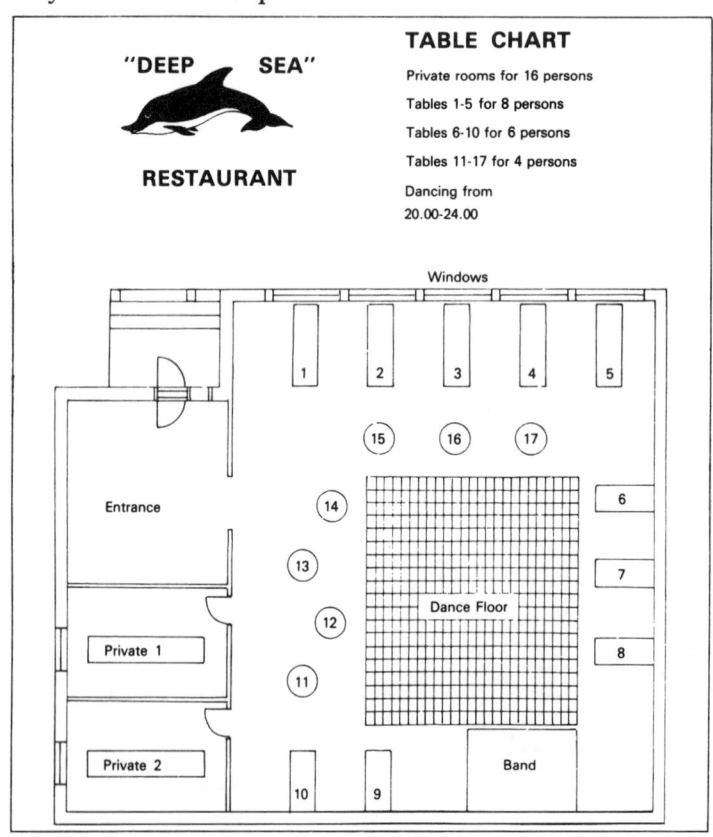

12 Work with a partner. Take turns to be A, a customer, or B, a waiter/waitress, at a restaurant you both choose. As A, you should first make notes about the kind of booking you want to make; as B, be prepared to ask questions politely. Use the chart in Exercise 7 to help you.

13 Look at the table chart of the Deep Sea Restaurant. You will see that there are two private rooms for a maximum of 16 people, five tables for 8, five tables for 6, and seven tables for 4. Then look at the reservations chart for Wednesday August 4th. You will see that some of the tables are already booked. Take turns to be customers ringing to make reservations, and staff accepting reservations and entering the names on the reservations chart. You can also use language from Unit 1, to ask questions and give information about services and amenities.

14 Work in the same way with the reservations chart of a restaurant that you know.

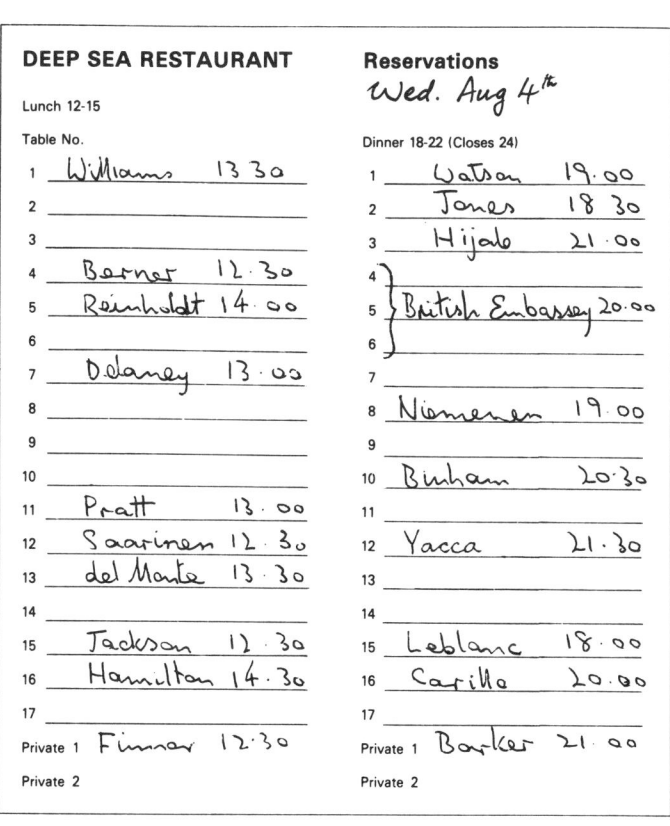

DEEP SEA RESTAURANT

Lunch 12-15

Table No.

1 Williams 13 30
2
3
4 Berner 12.30
5 Reinholdt 14.00
6
7 Delaney 13.00
8
9
10
11 Pratt 13.00
12 Saarinen 12.30
13 del Monte 13.30
14
15 Jackson 12.30
16 Hamilton 14.30
17
Private 1 Finner 12.30
Private 2

Reservations
Wed. Aug 4th

Dinner 18-22 (Closes 24)

1 Watson 19.00
2 Jones 18 30
3 Hijab 21.00
4 ⎫
5 ⎬ British Embassey 20.00
6 ⎭
7
8 Niemenen 19.00
9
10 Binham 20.30
11
12 Yacca 21.30
13
14
15 Leblanc 18.00
16 Carillo 20.00
17
Private 1 Barker 21.00
Private 2

Language reference

Days
today, tomorrow, on (Friday)

Times
(See Unit 1, page 9)

Spelling names
double L; hyphen; new word.

To make clear what letters one is saying, one can use either of these systems:

A as in Alpha	A for Andrew
B Bravo	B Benjamin
C Charlie	C Charlie
D Delta	D David
E Echo	E Edward
F Foxtrot	F Frederick
G Golf	G George
H Hotel	H Harry
I India	I Isaac
J Juliette	J Jack
K Kilo	K King
L Lima	L Lucy
M Mike	M Mary
N November	N Nellie
O Oscar	O Oliver
P Papa	P Peter
Q Quebec	Q Queenie
R Romeo	R Robert
S Sierra	S Sugar
T Tango	T Tommy
U Uniform	U Uncle
V Victor	V Victory
W Whisky	W William
X X-ray	X Xmas
Y Yankee	Y Yellow
Z Zulu	Z Zebra

For example:

West. Whisky – Echo – Sierra – Tango
West. W for William, E for Edward, S for sugar, T for Tommy.

Miscellaneous vocabulary
to book/reserve a table; to make a booking/reservation; a party (= a group of customers).

Requesting a reservation (*for comprehension*)
I'd like a table.
I'd like/I want to book/reserve a table.
Have you got/Do you have/Can I have a table?

Details of a reservation
a table for six (= *people*) for Thursday/tomorrow (= *day*) at 7.00 (= *time*) for Mr De Vienne (= *customer*).

Accepting a reservation
Certainly, Sir/Madam. (We can do that.)
Informal: Yes, that would be fine.
                Yes, we can/we have/you can/etc.

Polite questions about a customer's intentions, with *would*
For what day/time *would that be?*
Would that be for lunch or dinner?
How many *would there be* in your party?

Polite questions about a customer's wishes, with *would like*
Would you like a table near the band?

Polite requests, with *could* and *please*
Could I have your name, *please?*
Could you spell that, *please?*

Confirming a reservation
So that's a table for ... (*number of people*) for ... (*day*) at ... (*time*) for ... (*name*)
i.e. ... a table for six for Friday at 8 p.m. for Mr Smith.

Expressing pleasure about the reservation
We look forward to seeing you.

Reservations (2) Special wishes and some complications

To start you off

1 Sometimes, when customers ring to reserve a table, they have special wishes. Make a list of different kinds of requests they may make. For example: *1. A special diet.*

2 Make lists of foods which are: (a) dairy products, (b) shellfish, (c) mainly carbohydrate, (d) fatty. Use words in your own language if necessary.

3 What do you know about special diets? First, cover columns 2, 3 and 4, and discuss what foods are not allowed, or are allowed only in small quantities, in the diets which are listed in column 1.

1	2	3	4
Diet	**Only a little is allowed**	**None is allowed**	**This is necessary**
Slimmers	Fats and fatty foods; oils and oily foods; carbohydrates		
Vegetarian		Meat, fish	

Vegan		Meat, fish, eggs, dairy products	
Muslim		Pork, ham, bacon, shellfish, eels, alcohol	For many Muslims, animals must be killed according to religious ritual and under religious supervision (Halal meat).
Kosher (Jewish)		Pork, ham, bacon, shellfish, eels, fish without fins or scales	For many Jews, animals must be killed according to religious ritual and under religious supervision. Meat and dairy products must be kept separate. (They cannot be eaten at the same meal.)
Hindu		Beef, veal	
Diabetic	Carbohydrates		
For gastric ulcers	Fatty and oily foods	Alcohol, spicy foods	

Now study the whole table, and discuss which items on the menu below you would recommend to customers who are on the various diets.

Menu

Asparagus soup
Avocado pear with vinaigrette or prawns
Melon

* * *

Poached or grilled salmon
Roast pork
Grilled or fried steak
Vegetable lasagna
Mushroom omelette
Chicken salad
Cottage cheese salad

Potatoes (boiled, roast or fried)
Green beans, peas, carrots
Green salad

* * *

Apple pie with cream
Fruit salad with cream
Chocolate gateau
Crème caramel

[≈≈]

4A Study the sections **Special food**, **Special positions** and **Premises and furniture** on page 33. (Also, if you have not worked through Unit 1, study the section **Amenities and services** on page 8.)

Now listen to part A, in which five customers ring a restaurant. Note down in the appropriate columns what each customer wants.

Then listen to part B, in which the waiting staff reply to the customers.

If the staff can meet the request put a tick (√).
If they cannot meet it, put a cross (×).
If they cannot meet it but suggest an alternative, put a cross and an arrow (× →).

	Special food	Special position	Premises or furniture	Amenities
1.				*Am. Ex.* √
2.				
3.				
4.				
5.				

[≈≈]

4B Play the tape again. Study and practise the waiting staff's replies. Follow the procedure for Exercise 7 on page 4.

5 Look at these sentences. In each case, the waiter or waitress cannot meet the customer's request. Fill in the crossword to complete the sentences.

(a) We have no tables at that time. We're fully _____.
(b) We're in the basement, and there's no _____ (Am. E).
(c) There are five steps down to the restaurant, so there's no _____ for _____.
(d) We have no table big _____ for ten people.
(e) I'm sorry, you cannot smoke here. This is a _____-_____ area.
(f) We do not serve children's _____.

6

7 Work with a partner. Using the tables below, take turns to be A (a customer) or B (a waiter or waitress). A rings B and makes three requests each time. B can meet the first request (√), cannot meet the second (×), and cannot meet the third but suggests an alternative (× →).

Student A = Customer

R	I'd like (to book) a table	for ... (*number of people*)
E		on/for ... (*day*)
		at/for ... (*time*)
Q	Do you have any	vegetarian (etc.) dishes?
U		dishes suitable for ...?
E	We'd like a table	out of doors/near the window
		... (etc.)
S	Do you have	a lift/elevator?
T		any high chairs?
		... etc.

Student B = Server

Acknowledge-ment of request	√	(Yes,) certainly,/ No, Sir/Madam	(That would be no problem.) (You could ...)
Apology	×	(No,) I'm (very) sorry, Sir/Madam.	**Explanation** We're fully booked on .../at ... We have no ... There's no .../There are no ... We can't ... We don't ... We've run out of ...
Alternative	→	but we could you could you might like to	... ...

8   Study the section **Changing arrangements** on page 33. Six customers ring to make changes to their reservations. Match up the messages with their meanings. For example: *(a)* = 5.

Message

(a) I have a reservation for tomorrow. But I want to put it off.

(b) We're booked for 2.00. Could you put that forward to ...?

(c) There'll be nine of us instead of seven.

(d) We're booked for nine. Can we come at seven instead?

(e) We'd now like to come for dinner rather than lunch.

(f) We're going to have to postpone our reservation for tomorrow to Saturday.

(g) Now we'd rather come for lunch than dinner.

Meaning

(1) I want to come at seven o'clock.

(2) I want to come earlier than that.

(3) I want to come for lunch.

(4) I want to come for dinner.

(5) I want to come on a later day. (*Two messages mean this.*)

(6) There will be nine customers.

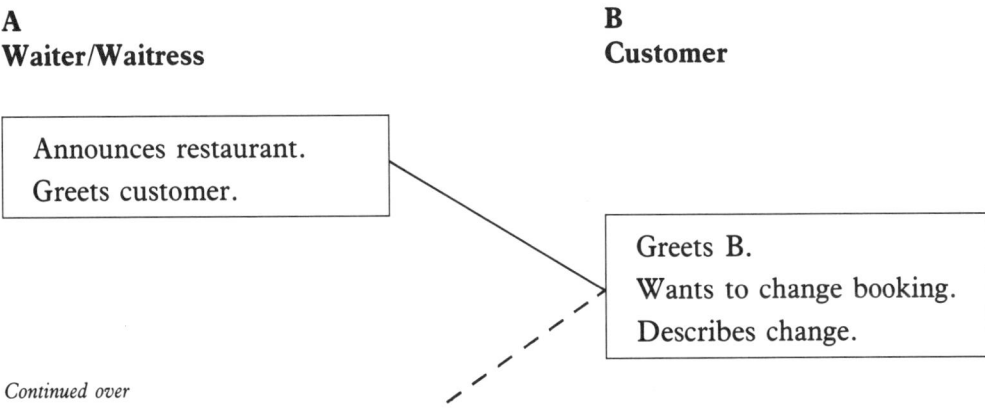

9A You will hear six customers telephoning to change their arrangements. First, decide what sort of change they want, and tick the appropriate box. Then listen again and write down what each customer wants.

	Cancel booking	Change table	Change day	Change time	Change number of people
(1)	☐	☐ _____	☐ _____	☐ _____	☑ 6 _____
(2)	☐	☐ _____	☐ _____	☐ _____	☐ _____
(3)	☐	☐ _____	☐ _____	☐ _____	☐ _____
(4)	☐	☐ _____	☐ _____	☐ _____	☐ _____
(5)	☐	☐ _____	☐ _____	☐ _____	☐ _____
(6)	☐	☐ _____	☐ _____	☐ _____	☐ _____

9B Listen to the waiters replying to the first four customers. Follow the procedure for Exercise 7 on page 4.

10 Work with a partner. Take turns to be A (a waiter or waitress) and B (various customers). Follow the chart below and use language from this Unit and Unit 3 to practise telephone conversations about changes of booking plans. B should first make notes about the changes she/he wants. A should sometimes meet the request, and sometimes not.

A
Waiter/Waitress

B
Customer

Announces restaurant.
Greets customer.

Greets B.
Wants to change booking.
Describes change.

Continued over

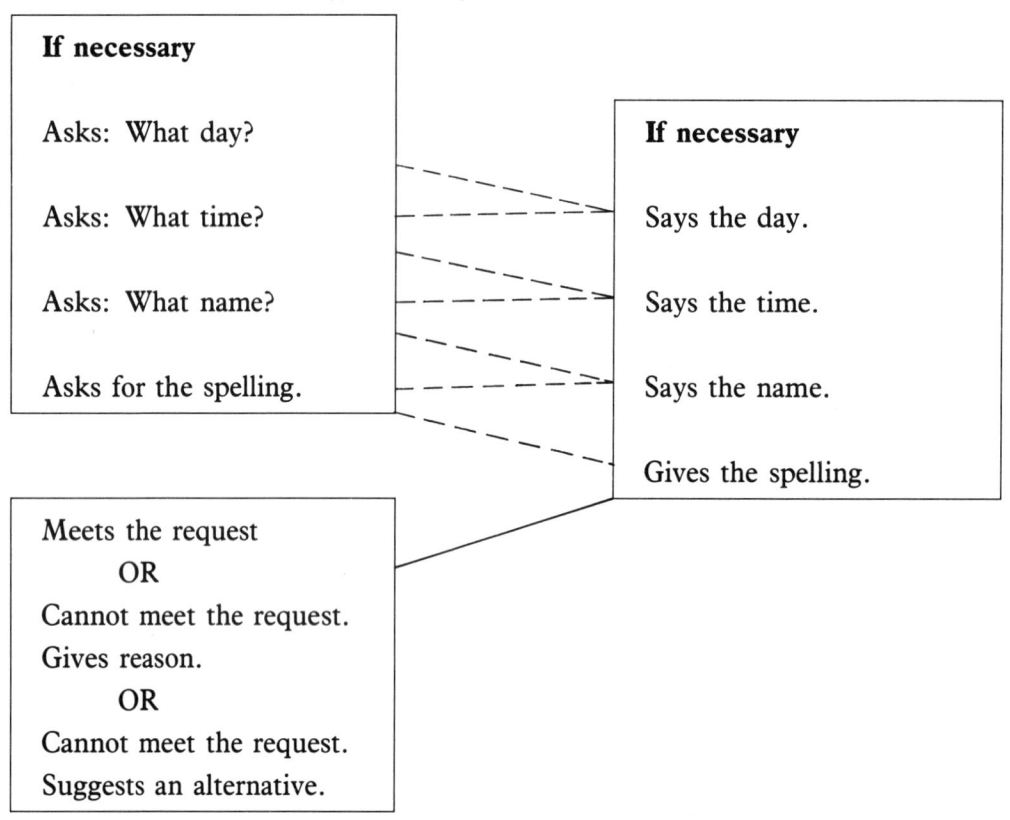

Follow-up

11 With a partner or in a group, plan suitable menus for some of the diets listed in Exercise 3.

12 Work with a partner. Take turns to be A (a waiter/waitress) and B (various customers). Use the table chart and reservations chart for the Deep Sea Restaurant on pages 22 and 23 or the charts of a restaurant in your locality. B should telephone to (a) make reservations, (b) to change reservations, or (c) make special requests. A can sometimes meet the requests, sometimes not, and can sometimes suggest alternatives. A should enter any bookings and changes of bookings on the reservations chart.

Language reference

Special food
vegetarian, vegan; Muslim, Halal, Kosher, Hindu; diabetic, diabetes; slimmer's (dieter's/weight watcher's) menu, fat-free; children's menu/portions. I have an allergy to (fish)/I am allergic to (fish).

Special positions
out of doors, in the shade/sun, on the terrace, . . .; near/by a window, with a view; by a window/the pool; near/not near the band/the dance floor/. . .; in the non-smoking section/area.

Premises and furniture
steps, stairs; the basement; a lift (Am.E = an elevator); access for wheelchairs/ wheelchair access; a high chair; air-conditioning.

Miscellaneous
suitable, extra

Meeting requests when answering a *Yes/No* question
Certainly, Sir/Madam. (That would be no problem.)
Informal: (Yes,) you could/there is/etc. (*'short answers'*)
         (Yes,) that's no problem/that would be no problem.

Meeting requests when responding to a statement
Formal: Very good, Sir/Madam.
Informal: That'll be fine./No problem!

Not meeting a request
I'm (very) sorry, Sir/Madam. We have no . . ./there's no . . ./ We can't . . ./ We don't . . ./We don't have any . . .
We're fully booked on that day/at that time.
We're closed on Monday.
We have no table big enough for sixteen (people).

Making suggestions
(but) you could . . ./ we could . . .

Changing arrangements (for comprehension)
to cancel; to postpone/put off . . . until/to . . . (= to change to a later time or day)
to put/bring . . . forward to . . . (= to change to an earlier time or day)
We'd rather come for dinner (than lunch) (= We want to come for dinner, not lunch.)
We'd like to come for dinner *instead of/rather than* lunch. (= We want to come for dinner, not lunch.)

UNIT 5

Directions for finding a restaurant

To start you off

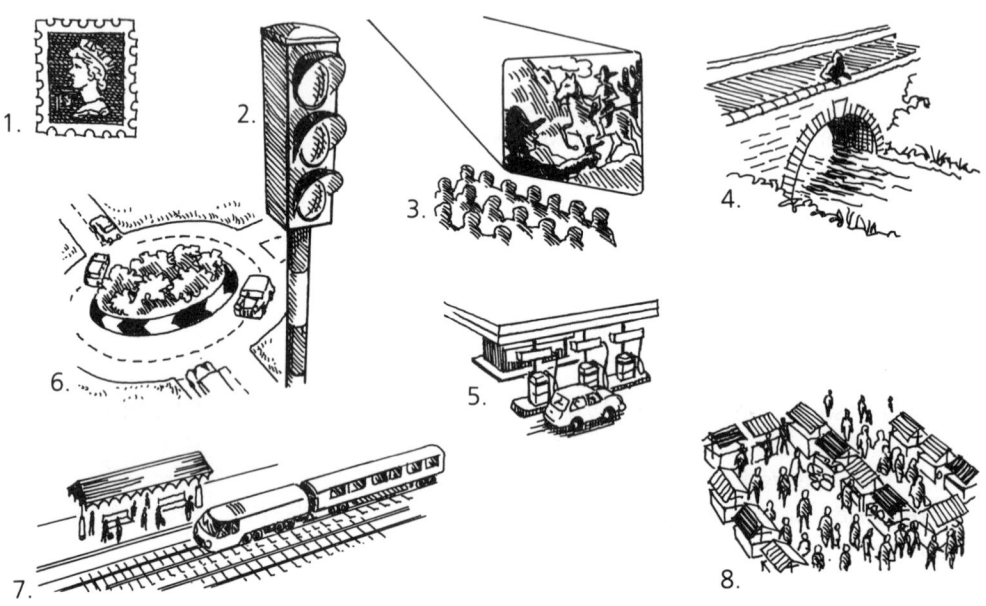

1   These pictures represent eight of the landmarks that are listed in the Language Reference section at the end of this Unit. Can you match the pictures and words? For example: *Picture 1 = Post office.*

2   Which of the places, buildings, etc. in the pictures above can one find near your college or restaurant? What other landmarks can one find near your college or restaurant?

3   Can you describe the position of your college, or of a restaurant that you know, using some of these expressions?

(a) not far from

(b) very near

(c) in (*name of street*)/on (*a road in the country*)

(d) opposite

(e) behind

(f) between

(g) next to

(h) about (a kilometre, etc.) from

(i) on the same side of the street/ road as

(j) on the opposite side of the street/ road to

(k) on the corner of

Developing the topic

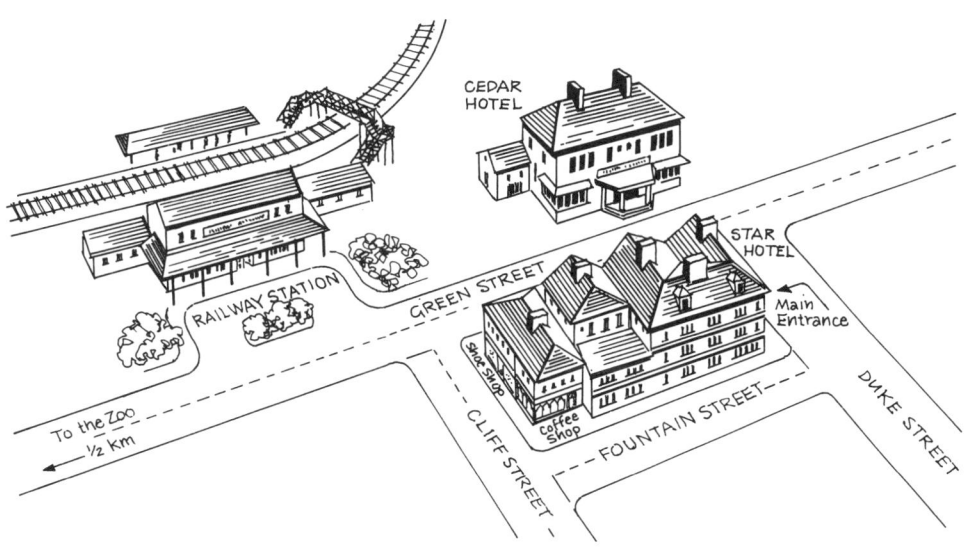

4   This map shows you the position of the Star Hotel. Complete the description of the hotel's position, using words from the list in Exercise 3. Use a different word or expression each time. You will hear the description in Exercise 5.

The hotel is *not far from* the zoo; it's about half a kilometre _____ the zoo, and it's very _____ the station. It's _____ the Cedar Hotel, but the entrance is _____ Duke Street. The Coffee Shop is _____ the corner _____ Cliff Street and Fountain Street. There is a shoe shop _____ the Coffee Shop.

5 Play the tape and check your answers to Exercise 4. Then play the tape again while you look at the map. Stop the tape at suitable points, and repeat the waitress's words.

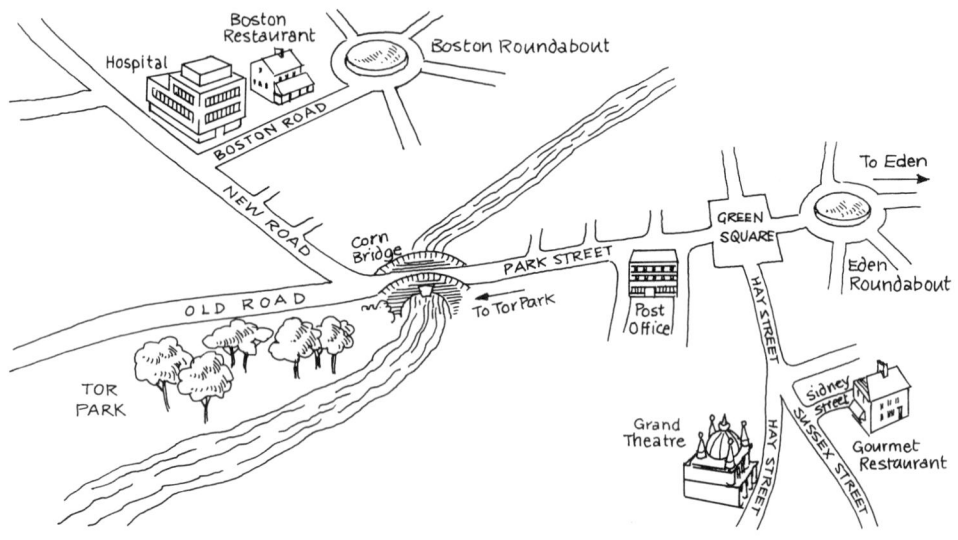

6 A waitress in the Boston Restaurant is giving directions on the telephone to a customer who is coming from the Grand Theatre. Write in the names of the landmarks, streets, etc. which the waitress mentions. You will hear the directions in Exercise 7.

'When you leave the theatre, turn left, and go along *Hay Street*. Go straight on as far as _____, then turn left into _____. Go past the _____ on your left, and go straight on, in the direction of _____. You'll cross _____, and just after that, the road forks. Take the right fork; you'll now be in _____. Then take the third turning on your right; that's _____. You'll see the restaurant on your left. It's just after the _____ and just before the _____.'

7 Play the tape and check your answers to Exercise 6. Then follow the same procedure as in Exercise 5.

8   With a partner, plan and write down directions for someone who wants to get from the hospital to the Gourmet Restaurant. Begin: 'When you leave the hospital . . .' Mention these places in your directions:

(a) New Road
(b) Corn Bridge
(c) Park Street
(d) Eden
(e) The Post Office
(f) Green Square
(g) The Eden Roundabout
(h) Hay Street
(i) Sussex Street
(j) Sidney Street

Then, with your partner, join another pair of students. Read aloud and compare your directions and theirs, for each stage of the journey, one stage at a time. Discuss the different sets of directions and decide which is better.

9   With a partner or in a group, plan and write down directions for two people coming to your college (or to a restaurant that you know) from two different places. Then read aloud and compare your directions with those of other students.

Follow-up

10   Play a game like this: one student thinks of a restaurant (or a well-known building, monument, etc.) in your locality, but does not name it. The other students ask 'Yes/No' questions about its position.

For example: *'Is it near . . . ? Is it in . . . ?'* The first student can only answer *'Yes'* or *'No'*. The other students must try to guess the place in ten questions or less.

11   Work with a partner, in a group or with the whole class. Take turns to give directions, like this:

Think of a restaurant (or a well-known building, monument, etc.) in your locality, but don't name it. Give directions on how to get there from a place which you name (for example the railway station). Your partner or partners make notes or draw a rough map while you speak; they can ask questions, correct your directions, etc. If the whole class does this exercise, one student can sketch the map on the board, while the rest of the class watch, comment and ask questions. As the journey proceeds, students try to guess where they are going.

Language reference

Landmarks

a post office, a cinema (Am.E = movie theater), a petrol station (Am.E = gas station), a (railway) station, a market, a hospital, a theatre (Am.E = theater), a zoo, a shoe/flower/etc. shop, a·bridge, a police station, a block of flats, a sky scraper, a school, a fire station, a park, an apartment building, a department store

Streets and roads

a street (*usually in a town or village*), a road (*usually wide and long, and going from one town to another*), a turning, a fork, a roundabout (Am.E = traffic circle)

Ordinal numbers

first, second, third, fourth, fifth, sixth, seventh, etc.

Cardinal points

north, south, east, west, north-east/west, south-east/west

Verbal expressions

cross, go straight on, take the second turning, turn left into, you'll see the restaurant on your left

Prepositions etc. describing position

in (Am.E = on) Duke Street, opposite, next to, not far from, (about) a kilometre from, near, on the corner of, on your left/right, just before/after the roundabout

Prepositions etc. describing direction

from, to, along, past, in the direction of, as far as, turn into Green Street

Receiving customers and taking orders

To start you off

1 List the order in which restaurant staff do these things. For example: *1 = (e)*

(a) ask if guest would like to see the wine list
(b) bring the wine list
(c) serve bread or rolls
(d) take guests to their table
(e) receive guests when they arrive
(f) take guests coats to the cloakroom
(g) take down the orders for the first and second courses
(h) ask if guests would like an *apéritif* (a drink before a meal)
(i) offer water
(j) take down the wine order
(k) bring the menu

Who would do each of these jobs?

2 Below are the courses on two kinds of menu, but they are in the wrong order. Put the courses in a better order, and discuss what dishes etc. one might serve for some of them. For example: *1. Hors d'oeuvres: eggs mayonnaise . . . .*

A la carte menu in a four-star restaurant: Cheese board – Entrées – Coffee and mints – Cold platters – Sweets – Hors d'oeuvre – Fish – Soups – Vegetables

Coffee-shop menu in an international hotel: Wine list – Main dishes – Soups – Desserts – Sandwiches – Appetizers – Beverages – Pasta dishes – Cold plate

3 Two customers have arrived for dinner. Complete the waiter's sentences. You will hear them in Exercise 4.

1: Good - - - - - - -, Sir. Do you have a r - - - - v - - - - -?
2. C - - - - I have your n - - -, pl - - - -?
3. C - - I t - - - your c - - - s?
4. W - - - - you l - - - an ap - - - t - f before your m - - -?
5. H - - - is the menu, Sir.
6. W - - - - you l - - - to or - - - now, Sir?

Developing the topic

4 Listen to the conversation between the waiters and the customers. First check your answers to Exercise 3. Then listen again. Put √, × or ? in this table to show the customer's responses, and add any details.

	Yes	**No**	**Has not decided**	**Details**
Reservation?	✓			*For two*
Name?				
Coats to cloakroom?				
Apéritifs?				
Ice?				
Water?				
Ready to order?				

5 Study and then practise the waiters' sentences. Follow the procedure for Exercise 7 on page 4.

6   First, study the following:

Would you like *a* table near the window?
Would you like *some* water?

Use *a/an* before 'countable' nouns in the singular	Use *some* before 'uncountable' nouns
a table, chair, parasol, drink, starter, roll, salad *an* apéritif, ash tray (*an* if the next word begins with *a, e, i, o* or *u*) All these nouns are 'countable': they can be in the plural; e.g. *two tables, three apéritifs*.	*some* water, wine★, ice, bread, butter, soup, coffee, beer★, jam, honey, sauce, meat, fish, cheese, fruit. These nouns cannot be in the plural. Liquids and substances are usually 'uncountable'.
Use *some* before 'countable' nouns in the plural	
some rolls, ash trays	

Note: It is not always easy to know if a noun is 'countable' or 'uncountable'. For example, *roll* is 'countable' but *bread* is 'uncountable'. So it is best to learn this vocabulary with *a* or *some* before each word.

7   Now work with a partner. Take turns to be A (a waiter/waitress) or B (a customer). Use the table below to ask questions and respond, like this:

A. Would you like some water, Sir?
B. Some water? Not really, thanks.
A. Very good, Sir.
   (Informal: Right!)

A. Waiter			B. Customer	A. Waiter
Would you like	a/an	apéritif? …?	(Repeats the offer) (Yes,) please.	Very good, Sir/Madam. (*Informal:* Fine!/OK)
	some	water? …?.	(Yes,) OK. (Yes,) fine.	
Would you like to		sit near …? sit in the shade/sun? see the wine list/ set menu? order now?	Sure. That would be nice/great/ splendid/etc. Yes, I could do with a/some … No, thanks. No, thanks. Not really, (thanks) (No,) it's OK. I don't know. I'm not too sure. Let me see/think. Can you give us a bit more time?	Certainly, Sir/Madam. (*Informal:* Sure!/OK!)
Would you like to		come this way?*	Sure/fine/OK/Yes.	

*This is not really a question, but a polite request. It means: *Please come this way.*

[tape icon]

8 Study the menu on pages 44 and 45 first. Then listen. You will hear a waiter taking down the order from two customers. Write down their order.

	Woman	Man
Starter		
Main course		
Extras		
Wine		

Study and then practise the waiter's sentences. Follow the procedure for Exercise 7 on page 4.

9   Work with a partner. Use the menu on page 44 and take turns to be A (a customer who wants some advice) and B (a waiter/waitress).

A

I haven't decided I can't make up my mind I'm wondering	about	an appetizer a soup a main course a dessert
What would you suggest What do you recommend	as	

B

I can recommend the	...	It's They're	excellent particularly good one of the chef's specialities

10   Work with a partner. Take turns to be A (a customer) and B (a waiter/waitress).

A

I'd like I'll have	(a) soup the fresh salmon the grilled steak a cold platter a side salad

B

Very good, Sir/Madam. (*Informal*: Right!)			
Would you like the	vegetable soup poached salmon fillet steak roast beef green salad	or the	consommé? ...

A
Oh, the . . . , please.

WALTHAM FOREST COLLEGE

Training Restaurant

The Mallinson Room

Appetisers

Smoked haddock croquettes
Smoked Scotch salmon
Honeydew melon
Avocado pear vinaigrette

Soups

Country vegetable soup
Beef consommé with rice

Fish

Fresh salmon, poached or grilled, with new potatoes
Grilled or fried Dover sole, with fried potatoes,
Tartare sauce

Entrées

Roast saddle of lamb, with red currant jelly
Poached breast of chicken with cream, almonds and rice
Grilled fillet or sirloin steak

Fresh vegetables

Carrots — French beans — peas — broccoli — grilled mushrooms
Potatoes: boiled — roast — fried — sauté

Cold platters

Roast beef with horseradish
Duck with pâté and cherries
Choice of salads: green, mixed

Desserts

Chocolate brandy cake
Cherry and almond tart
Lemon mousse
Cream caramel
Fresh fruit salad and cream

Cheeseboard

Cheddar, Stilton, Brie, Emmenthal, served with crackers and celery

Coffee, mints

A selection of recommended wines from our cellar

House wines

Mallinson rouge
Mallinson blanc

Champagne

Bollinger non vintage

Sparkling

Asti Spumante

Red Burgundy

Moulin au Vent 1986
Côtes de Beaune Villages 1984
Nuits St Georges Les Caillerets 1982

White Burgundy

Chablis La Fourchaume 1986
Pouilly Fuissé 1986

Rosé

Taval, from the Rhône Valley

Red Bourdeaux

St Emilion 1986
Côtes de Bourg AC 1985
Médoc AC 1984

White Bourdeaux

Château Oliver 1985
Sauternes AC 1986

German wines, Hock & Mosel

Hans Christof 1987
Bereich Nierstein 1988
Bereich Bernkastel 1987

[ᴏᴏ]

11 You will hear seven customers making requests to a waiter. Note down each request, and indicate the waiter's responses, like this:

√ = Yes.   ? = I don't know.
× = No.   × → = No, but instead ...

	The customer wants	**The waiter replies**
1.	Fried potatoes with poached salmon	√
2.		
3.		
4.		
5.		
6.		
7.		

[ᴏᴏ]

Study and then practise the waiter's replies. Follow the procedure for Exercise 7 on page 4.

12 Match up the wines in the first column with the dishes in the last column. Then practise making recommendations, like this:

I'd suggest a medium dry white wine to go with the haddock croquettes, Sir/Madam.

I'd (= I would) suggest a			
medium sweet white sweet white medium dry white dry white sparkling light red full-bodied red rosé	wine	to go with the	haddock croquettes. smoked salmon. fresh salmon. Dover sole. roast lamb. poached chicken. steak. duck salad. cheese.

13 Practise describing the wines on the Mallinson Room menu or wines from your region, using the expressions in the table above. For example: *St. Emilion is a full-bodied red wine.*

14 Ask and answer questions about wines on the menu or from your region, like this:

Customer

What's	the difference between	the	Beaujolais	and the	Nuits St. Georges?
Which is	lighter: more full-bodied: drier: sweeter:	the	Beaujolais . . .	or the	Nuits St. Georges? . . .

Waiter/waitress

Oh, the	Beaujolais . . .	is	lighter etc.	than the	Nuits St. Georges. . . .

or:

Oh, the	Nuits St. Georges . . .	is not as	light etc.	as the	Beaujolais. . . .

Follow-up

15 Rôle-play in groups. Waiters or waitresses receive customers, take them to their tables, offer and bring apéritifs, etc., and bring the menu. The customers respond. Use the language in Exercises 6 and 8.

16   Work in pairs. Take turns to be A (a customer) and B (a waiter or waitress). Use the menu on pages 44 and 45 to practise making recommendations, like this:

A	**B**
I'm/My friend is — diabetic — slimming/dieting — on a low-fat diet — a Muslim — Jewish — a Hindu I have/My friend has — an ulcer I'm a vegetarian — not very hungry — very thirsty — allergic to nuts — in a rush I don't like cheese horseradish etc.	In that case, Sir/Madam, I'd suggest the ..., then the ... (with/without ...), and for a dessert the ... (with/without the ...)

17   Rôle-play in groups. Use your own menu or the menu on pages 44 and 45, to practise giving and taking orders. Include customers who ask for advice or have special wishes, and situations where dishes are not available.

Language reference

Restaurant staff
owner, manager, chef, cook, head waiter/maître d'hôtel, waiter/waitress (Am.E = (food) server), wine waiter/waitress, cashier, barman/bartender

Parts of a menu
starters (Brit.E)/appetizers, hors d'oeuvre, soup; eggs; pasta; fish; main dishes, entrées, grills, grilled meat or fish (Am.E), roasts; vegetables; poultry or game; cold platters, salads; desserts/sweets; cheeses, the cheese board; coffee, beverages; wines, apéritifs (cocktails)

Describing steaks
(very) rare, medium rare; medium; (very) well done

Describing wines
sweet, medium sweet; dry, medium dry; light; full-bodied; fruity; sparkling; the house wine

Drinks other than wines: see Unit 10: **Drinks**

Wine containers
a bottle, a half-bottle, a carafe

'Countable' and 'Uncountable' nouns
a roll, *an* apéritif; *some* rolls ('countable' − plural) *some* water ('uncountable')

Comparisons
The Beaujolais is *lighter than* the Nuits St Georges. The Nuits St Georges is *more full-bodied than* the Beaujolais. The Nuits St Georges is *not as light as* the Beaujolais.

Polite questions with *would you like . . .?*
Would you like some water?
Would you like to see the wine list?

Asking about choices
Have you chosen your wine?
Which wine would you like to go with your lamb?
How would you like your steak?

A polite request
Would you like to come this way, Sir?

Polite expressions
When bringing something: The menu, Sir. Your soup, Madam.
When bringing something that the customer has just asked for: (Could we have an ash tray?) Certainly, Madam. Here's an ash tray.

Polite responses
(We'd like to sit near the window.) Very good, Sir.
(Can we sit near the window?) Certainly, Sir.
(*Informal:* Fine!/OK/Right!)

Recommendations
I can recommend the salmon. (= It's very good.)
I'd (= I would) suggest the St. Emilion to go with your lamb. (= It's suitable.)

Explaining prices: See Unit 11: **Talking about money**

Explaining dishes: Starters and main courses

To start you off

1 In the table below are eleven types of ingredients. From the list, find one other ingredient of each type.

turkey – mustard – beans – kidney – herbs – margarine – rice – salmon – lobster – pheasant – lamb

vegetables	fish	shellfish	poultry	game
cauliflower *beans*	trout	crab	duck	venison

offal	meat	cereals and cereal products		fats & oils
liver	beef	flour		butter

condiments	flavourings
pepper	garlic

How many more ingredients of each type can you name? (You will find lists of ingredients in Appendix 3, on pages 154—173.)

2 Which verb goes with which picture?

to chop — to fillet — to grate — to mash — to mince — to shred — to slice — to stuff — to peel

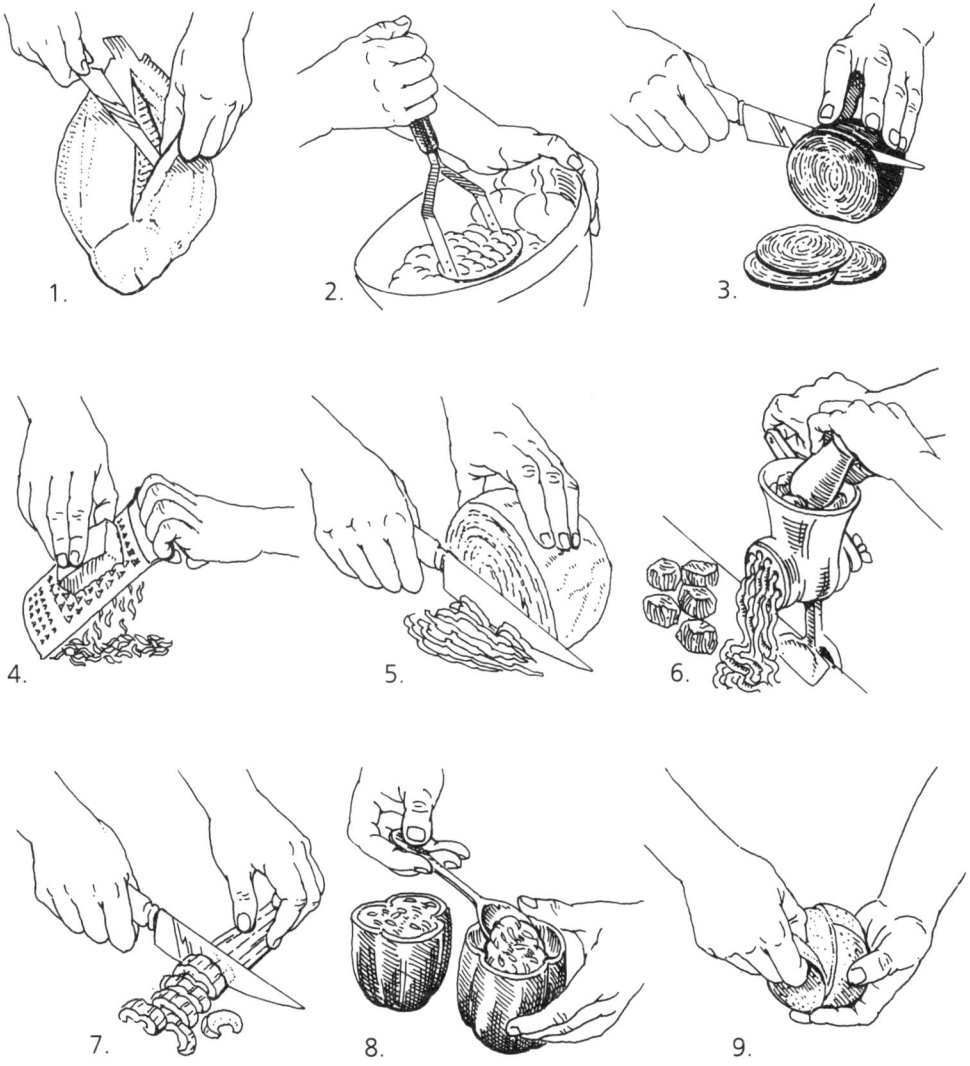

1.

2.

3.

4.

5.

6.

7.

8.

9.

3 Methods of cooking: find the correct name to go with each definition. For example: *(a) = (ii)*.

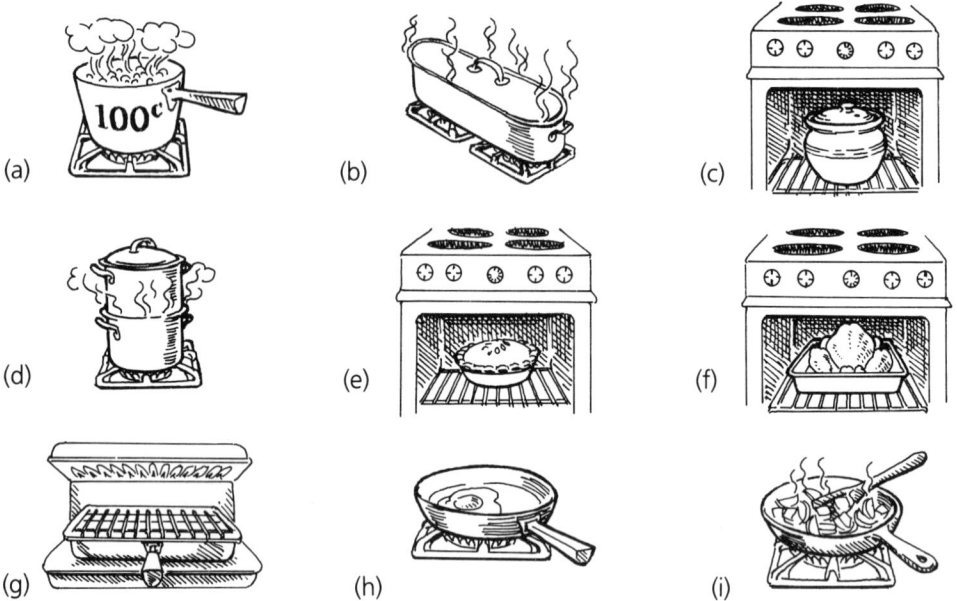

Method of cooking

(a) in water or another liquid at 100°C
(b) in water or another liquid at a little less than 100°C
(c) in water or another liquid at 100°C, slowly and for a long time (e.g. beef)
(d) in steam
(e) in the oven, with very little or no fat (e.g. bread)
(f) in the oven, with fat (e.g. meat)
(g) under (or over) direct heat (e.g. steak)
(h) in fat or oil
(i) in a little fat, for a short time

Name

(i) to bake
(ii) to boil
(iii) to fry
(iv) to grill (Am.E = broil)
(v) to poach
(vi) to roast
(vii) to sauté
(viii) to steam
(ix) to stew

4 Name:

(a) foods or dishes which are: cold − hot* − raw − cooked − spicy − salty − sour − rich light
(b) soups which are: thick − clear − creamy

*Note: The word *hot* can also mean *very spicy*, full of pepper, etc. For example: *Would you like a hot curry or a mild one?*

Developing the topic

5 Work with a partner. Take turns to be A or B.

A should look at the list of verbs in Exercise 2.
B should look at the list of ingredients on pages 62−63 and the lists in Appendix 3 on pages 154−173.

A

What can chefs	grate? shred? ...?

B

They can	grate carrots. shred lettuce. ... ...

6 Work with a partner. Take turns to be A or B.

A should look at the list of cooking methods (i−ix) in Exercise 3.
B should look at the list of ingredients on pages 62−63.

(a) **A**

What can chefs	grill? fry? ...

B

They can	grill salmon, lobster, liver, ... fry onions, mushrooms, cod, ...

(b) **B**

How can chefs cook	salmon? onions? ...

A

They can	bake, grill or poach salmon. boil, fry, or sauté onions. etc.

7 When you explain a dish to customers, you need to tell them about:

— the main *ingredients*;
— how the chefs *prepare* the ingredients (e.g. *chop, slice, mince*)
— and how they *cook* the ingredients (e.g. *boil, fry*)

Complete the words in column 2.

The chefs do this	**The waiter or waitress serves this**
They:	
(a) mince beef	minced beef
(b) mash potatoes	m - - - - - potatoes
(c) shred cabbage	- - - - dd - - cabbage
(d) fillet plaice	- - - - - - - - plaice
(e) slice mushrooms	- - - - - - mushrooms
(f) fry scampi	- - ie - scampi
(g) stew lamb	- - - - - - lamb
(h) grill sardines	- - - - - - - sardines
(i) bake ham	- - - - - ham

Note
1. *Roast* does not take *ed*. *Sauté* can take *ed*. *Would you like roast chicken and sauté/sautéed potatoes?*
2. These words change their spelling:

   chop – chopped; shred – shredded; fry – fried.

8 Write down the four lists of words that you hear.

List 1	**List 2**	**List 3**
chopped onions	boiled _____	_____ sole
_____ _____	_____ _____	_____ _____
_____ _____	_____ _____	_____ _____
_____ _____	_____ _____	**List 4**
_____ _____	_____ _____	_____ _____
_____ _____		_____ _____

Check your lists with the tapescript on page 140.

9 Follow the procedure for Exercise 7 on page 4. Pronounce *ed* like this:

in List 1 − *t*;   in List 2 − *d*;   in List 3 − *id*.

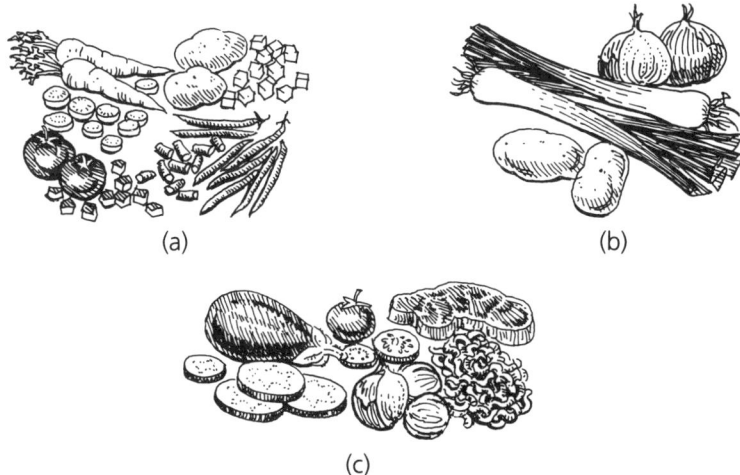

(a)   (b)

(c)

10 A waiter is describing *the main ingredients* in three dishes. Look at the pictures and complete his descriptions. You will hear them in Exercise 11.

(a) Salade breton con - - - - - of ch - pp - - c - - - - - -, French b - - - -, p - - - - - - - and t - - - - - -.
(b) Vichyssoise is m - - - of l - - - -, o - - - - - and p - - - - - - -.
(c) Moussaka is m - - - o - m - - - - - lamb, sl - - - - au - - - - - - - - -, o - - - - - and t - - - - - - -.

| oo |

11 Listen to the tape and check your answers to Exercise 10. Then listen again and fill in this chart.

General description of the dish	Additional ingredients	Other details
1 a salad	*with hard-boiled eggs ... and ...*	*The vegetables are not raw / are cooked*
2 *a cr... ...*	*with ...*	
3 *a sort of ...*		

12 Play the tape again, and follow the procedure for Exercise 7 on page 4.

13

	Type of dish			Main ingredients		Additional ingredients
It's a	-- cold rich ...	salad. soup. stew. ...	It's made from	raw chopped slices of ...	...	with	black olives. oil and garlic. red wine. ...

Work on your own or with a partner. Use the framework above, and words from the language reference section on pages 62–65, to write an explanation of:

(a) a salad
(b) a soup
(c) an appetizer
(d) a main dish
(e) a vegetable dish

Then, alone or with your partner, read each explanation to another student or group of students. They should try to guess what dish you are explaining. Together discuss the wording of your explanations.

The chefs fry the trout in butter.
They fry the mushrooms in oil.

The trout is fried in butter.
The mushrooms are fried in oil.

14   When waiters and waitresses explain a dish, they usually talk only about the food, not about the chefs. Change these sentences in the same way.

(a) The chefs cook the beef in wine.
    The beef is cooked in wine.
(b) They poach the cod in milk.
    The cod is ...
(c) They flavour the soup with herbs.
(d) They stuff the heart with bread, onions and nuts.
(e) They flavour the chicken with lemon.
(f) They serve the smoked salmon with brown bread and butter.
(g) They garnish the soup with small pieces of fried bread.
(h) They fry the vegetables in oil.
    The vegetables are ...
(i) They poach the poussins in wine.
    The poussins are ...
(j) They fill the pancakes with cream cheese.
(k) They flavour the dumplings with herbs.
(l) They stuff the tomatoes with fried ham and onion.
(m) They serve the shrimps on a bed of lettuce.

15

no wine   very little wine   a little wine   some wine   a lot of wine

Uncountable ingredients.

. . .	has	no	wine	in it.
	contains	very little (just) a little quite a lot of a lot of	butter garlic . . .	

no olives   very few olives   a few olives   some olives   a lot of olives

Countable ingredients.

. . .	has	no	olives	in it.
	contains	very few (just) a few quite a lot of a lot of	prawns . . .	

Practise describing various dishes like this. For example: *Boeuf bourguignon has quite a lot of wine in it. It contains some herbs.*

16 Explaining a dish. Choose phrases from B in the chart below to explain Tortilla. Here is the information you need:

Tortilla: a sort of omelet
Main ingredients: eggs and potatoes
Additional ingredients: onion (just a little)
Preparation: slice potatoes, chop onion
Method of cooking: fry in oil
Accompaniment: serve with a green salad.

A: Customer	B: Waiter or waitress

A: Customer	B: Waiter or waitress
What's ...? What's this dish here? Can you tell me about this?	
	Tortilla, Sir/Madam? It's a sort of ... It consists of ... and sliced ... with some ... It's fried in ...
Is there a lot of onion in it? How much onion is there in it? Does it contain any garlic? Is there any flour in it?	
	It contains ... onion. It contains no ...
What's it served with? What does it come with? Is there anything to go with it? Does it come with a salad?	
	(No,) it's served on its own. (No,) it comes with ... (Yes,) it's served ...

17   Work with a partner. A should read the information below. B should read the information on page 152.

Student A

(a) You are a waiter/waitress. B, a customer, will ask you questions about Ratatouille. Use the waiter's words in Exercise 16 to help you explain it.

   Ratatouille: a sort of vegetable stew.
   Main ingredients: tomatoes, aubergines, green peppers, courgettes.
   Additional ingredients: oil, butter, garlic.
   Preparation: slice main ingredients.
   Method of cooking: sauté and then stew slowly in the oven.
   Accompaniment: serve with boiled potatoes or rice.

(b) You are a customer. Use the customer's words in Exercise 16 to help you ask B about Wiener Schnitzel.

Follow-up

18   Work with a partner who speaks your language. Take turns to be A or B.

(a) A should say the names of ingredients in your language. B should say their names in English.
(b) Work in the same way, but A should say how ingredients have been prepared or cooked. For example: *chopped liver, baked cod, etc.*

19   Work with a partner. Take turns to be A (a customer) and B (a waiter/waitress). A asks B to explain the items in bold type in column 1. B finds the correct explanation in column 2 and gives it. For example:

A. *What's a chowder?*
B. *It's a thick soup with large pieces of fish in it.*

fish **chowder**	a clear soup
lobster **bisque**	a thick soup with large pieces of ... in it
hors d'oeuvre	small portions of various savoury dishes
beef **consommé**	a thick, creamy soup
croûtons	small pieces of fried bread

Then make a list of other usual items on a menu, and practise giving similar explanations.

20   The words in bold type in Column 1 refer to some classic ways of preparing food. Work with a partner. Take turns to be A (a customer) and B (a waiter/waitress). A asks B to explain the preparation of the dishes. B uses the notes in column 2 to reply. For example:

A. *What does curry mean?*
B. *It means that the chicken is cooked in a thick, spicy sauce.*

Dish	Method of preparation
chicken **curry**	cook in thick, spicy sauce
scrambled eggs	stir and cook in butter
cauliflower **au gratin**	cover with sauce, sprinkle with breadcrumbs and cheese, then brown in oven or under grill
fricassé of veal	stew pieces, serve in thick, creamy sauce
trout **meunière**	cook in butter, serve with lemon and parsley
beef **hamburger**	mince beef, grill or fry, serve in a soft bun
ham **omelet**	whisk eggs, cook in butter, add pieces of ham

Then with your partner, make a list of other usual methods of preparation. Take turns to ask about them and to explain them. For example: *What does 'chasseur' mean? It means that the (chicken) is cooked with mushrooms, shallots and white wine.*

21   Work with a partner. Take turns to be A (a customer) and B (a waiter/waitress). B writes down the name of an appetizer, a soup and a main dish. A asks for information about the dishes and B gives the information. Work as in Exercises 16 and 17.

22   A guessing game: one student starts describing a dish; the other student(s) call out the name of the dish as soon as they have guessed it.

Language reference (See pages 154–173 for more detailed lists, in English, French, Spanish, Italian, German and Greek.)

Ingredients

1. These words are 'uncountable', except where 'countable' is indicated.
2. However, it is possible to refer to some 'countable' ingredients as 'uncountable' if one is not thinking of them as whole items, but as portions, parts of a dish, flavourings, etc. For example:

Countable	Uncountable
boiled potatoes	Would you like some mashed potato? (= a portion)
grilled tomatoes	There's some tomato in the salad. (= pieces of tomato as part of the dish)
boiled onions	The soup is flavoured with onion.

Such 'countable' words are indicated by the symbol (+ *U*).

Vegetables

avocado (*countable* if one is talking about the whole fruit), beetroot, cabbage, cauliflower, lettuce

Countable, plural: aubergines (+ *U*) (Am.E = egg plant), beans, carrots, leeks, mushrooms, olives, onions (+ *U*), peas, green/red peppers, potatoes (+ *U*), tomatoes (+ *U*), turnips (+ *U*)

Sea fish
plaice, sole
Countable, plural: anchovies, sardines

Fresh water fish
carp, salmon, trout

Shellfish
crab, lobster
Countable, plural: prawns, scampi

Poultry
chicken, duck, turkey
Countable: poussin

Game
pheasant, rabbit, venison

Offal
liver (*countable, plural* for chicken livers), tongue
Countable, plural: hearts (+ *U*), kidneys

Meat
beef, lamb, pork, veal, ham

Dairy products
cheese, cream, milk

Cereals and cereal products
bread, rice, flour
Countable, plural: breadcrumbs

Fat and oils
butter, margarine, (olive, etc.) oil

Parts of eggs
egg yolk, egg white

Condiments
salt, pepper, mustard, vinegar

Flavourings
garlic, onion
Countable, plural: herbs, spices

Types of dishes
an hors d'oeuvre, an omelet/omelette, a pancake, a pie, a salad (+ *U*), a sandwich

Accompaniments
French dressing, mayonnaise, (tomato, etc.) sauce
Countable, plural: croutons, dumplings

Pieces of food (*countable*)
small/large pieces of meat, a slice of chicken, strips of ham; a chop, a cutlet, a fillet, a steak

Adjectives describing foods or dishes
cold, hot, raw, cooked, spicy, salty, sour, rich, heavy, light, creamy; clear soup, thick soup

Adjectives describing ingredients
fresh, smoked, tinned (Am.E = canned), mixed; hard-boiled eggs

Verbs describing ways of cutting
chop, cut, fillet, grate, mash, mince, shred, slice

Verbs describing ways of cooking
In water or other liquids: boil, braise, poach, stew
In steam: steam
In fat or oil: fry, sauté
In dry heat: bake, grill (Am.E = broil), roast

Compound nouns
wine sauce, lemon dressing, rice stuffing

Verbs with -ed for describing preparation and cooking
sliced mushrooms, stewed beef

The passive for explaining dishes
The cod is poached in milk. The tomatoes are stuffed with rice.

Expressions of quantity
For 'uncountable' ingredients: no, very little, (just) a little, some, quite a lot of, a lot of butter
For 'countable' ingredients: no, very few, (just) a few, some, quite a lot of, a lot of olives

Phrases describing the composition of dishes
It's a sort of pie.
It's like an omelet.
It contains flour.
It's made of fish and vegetables. It consists of fish and vegetables.
It's cooked in oil.
It's filled with cream. It's stuffed with rice.
It's flavoured with garlic.
It's garnished with tomatoes.
It's served with potatoes/on (a bed of) rice.

Questions about dishes (for comprehension)
Does it contain any garlic?
What's it served with?
Does it come with a salad?

During the meal

To start you off

1 Match the items and activities in the chart with the right number in the picture opposite.

Number	
_____	to carve
_____	to flambé
_____	to fillet
_____	a silver flat
_____	a vegetable dish
_____	a sauce boat
_____	a soup tureen
_____	a trolley
_____	a service counter
_____	a sideboard
_____	a hotplate

2 These are kinds of restaurant service. Match the definitions with the words underneath. For example: *(a)* = *4.*

(a) This is the highest level of service. The waiter/waitress serves the meal from a trolley or sidetable. He or she may need to fillet, carve, flambé, prepare or cook speciality dishes at the side table.

(b) Customers take a tray and move along a counter, choosing the dishes they want. The food may be ready on plates, or there may be staff who carve, service, etc.

(c) When the waiter/waitress collects the food from the kitchen, it is all ready on the customer's plate. He or she simply puts the plate in front of the customer.

(d) When the waiter/waitress collects the food from the kitchen, it is on silver flats, in entrée dishes, sauce boats, etc. He or she places the dishes on a hotplate or sideboard and then serves the food on the guests' plates, from each of the dishes in turn, using a spoon and fork.

(e) When the waiter/waitress collects the food, the main meat/fish dish is ready on the customer's plate, but the waiter/waitress serves the accompanying vegetables etc. from silver dishes.

(f) Waiters/waitresses serve the starters, dessert or cheese and coffee. The customers help themselves to the main course from a central area, often carving the meat from the joints themselves.

1. Full silver service
2. Plate service
3. Combined silver service and plate service
4. Guéridon service
5. Carvery service
6. Counter service

3 Can you name the restaurants in your locality which offer the different kinds of service listed above?

4 A customer who is enjoying a dish could use the words in column 1. Find words in column 2 which mean approximately the *opposite*. For example: *(a)* — *3*.

(a) delicious; excellent	1. sour
(b) tasty	2. dry
(c) juicy	3. awful, horrible, ghastly,
(d) fresh	revolting, terrible
(e) tender (meat)	4. stale, old, off
(f) sweet (fruit)	5. tasteless
	6. tough

Developing the topic

[cassette icon]

5   Six customers say what they want during the service of a meal. Put a tick (√) to show what each customer wants.

	Soup				Croutons			
	none	some	a little	a lot	none	some	a few	a lot
Customer 1	☐	☐	✔	☐	☐	☐	☐	☐
Customer 2	☐	☐	☐	☐	☐	☐	☐	☐
Customer 3	☐	☐	☐	☐	☐	☐	☐	☐
	Beef				Potatoes			
Customer 4	☐	☐	☐	☐	☐	☐	☐	☐
Customer 5	☐	☐	☐	☐	☐	☐	☐	☐
Customer 6	☐	☐	☐	☐	☐	☐	☐	☐

[cassette icon]

6   Customers from the tables call their waiter or waitress during a meal. Make a note of what each table wants.

1. Table 1. *rolls* _____
2. Table 2. _____
3. Table 3. _____
4. Table 4. _____
5. Table 5. _____

[cassette icon]

7   Study and then practise the staff's answers. Follow the procedure for Exercise 7 on page 4.

8   Work with a partner. Take turns to be A (a waiter/waitress) and B, C or D (three customers). Use the chart below to talk during a meal. Practise the three kinds of exchanges:

A – B – A1
A – C – A2
A – D – A3

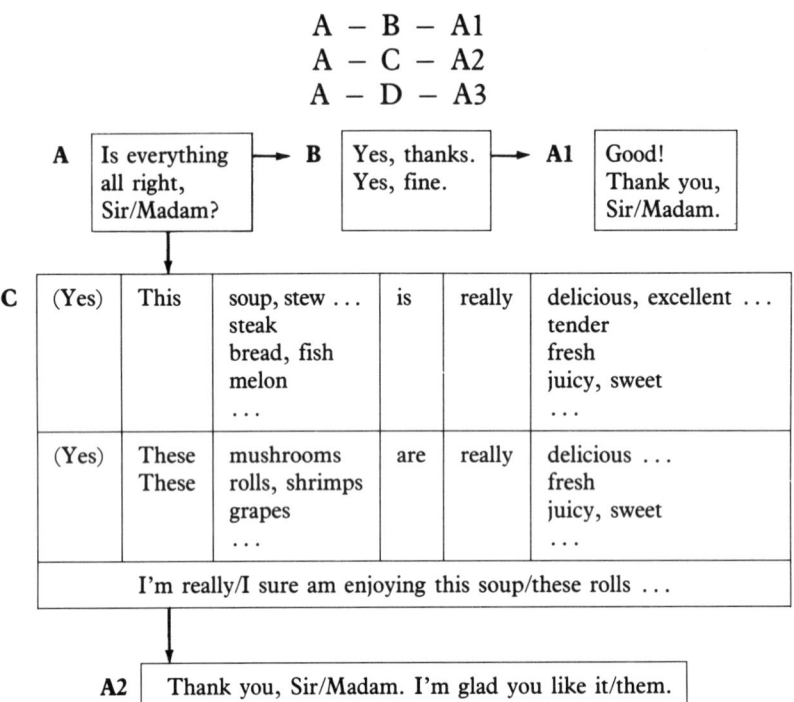

A | Is everything all right, Sir/Madam? → **B** | Yes, thanks. Yes, fine. → **A1** | Good! Thank you, Sir/Madam.

C

(Yes)	This	soup, stew ... steak bread, fish melon ...	is	really	delicious, excellent ... tender fresh juicy, sweet ...
(Yes)	These These	mushrooms rolls, shrimps grapes ...	are	really	delicious ... fresh juicy, sweet ...

I'm really/I sure am enjoying this soup/these rolls ...

A2 | Thank you, Sir/Madam. I'm glad you like it/them.

D

(No)	This	soup, stew ...	is	awful, disgusting, revolting, terrible
		steak bread fish milk ...	is	burnt, underdone, overdone, tough stale, dry, old off, not fresh off, sour bitter tasteless overcooked, undercooked too salty/spicy/peppery/sweet not spicy/sweet/... enough
	These	mushrooms ...	are	awful ... etc. (as above)

A3 | I'm *very* sorry, Sir/Madam.
Shall I take it/them away?
Would you like to order something else?
I'll bring you another .../some other ...

9   Think of suitable dishes to write in the last column. Then practise asking these questions. You can add local accompaniments and dishes for further practice.

Would you like	some	grated cheese ketchup mustard oil and vinegar horseradish sauce mayonnaise sauce tartare bread croutons wine . . .	to go with your	*soup?* . . .?
	a	roll		

10

another roll   **some more rolls**   **some more water**
(*'countable'*,   (*'countable'*,   (*'uncountable'*)
only one)   *several*)

Put *another* or *some more* in these sentences. Then practise saying them. Add local dishes for further practice.

(a) Would you like | . . . | potatoes?
(b)   salad?
(c)   bottle of wine?
(d)   mineral water?
(e)   finger bowl?
(f)   pot of coffee?
(g)   cream?
(h)   crackers?
(i)   bread?

Follow-up

11 Work in groups of three. Take turns to be A (the waiter or waitress) and B and C (two customers). Write out a menu, or use an available menu, and imagine that the meal is in progress. Practise these exchanges:

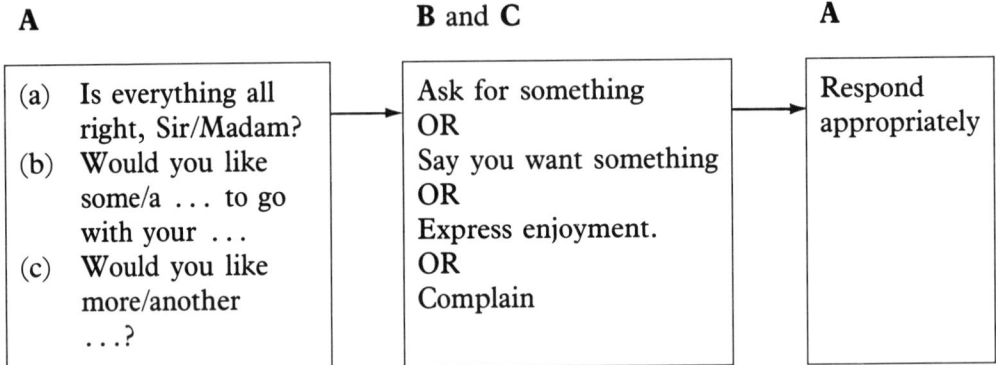

A	B and C	A
(a) Is everything all right, Sir/Madam? (b) Would you like some/a ... to go with your ... (c) Would you like more/another ...?	Ask for something OR Say you want something OR Express enjoyment. OR Complain	Respond appropriately

Use the language in Exercises 5–10.

Language reference

Words for describing different kinds of service
guéridon service (Am.E = French service)
silver service (Am.E = Russian service), plate service (Am.E = American service),
carvery service, cafeteria/counter service

Equipment
a trolley, a service counter, a sideboard, a side table, a hotplate
a silver flat (Am.E = platter), a vegetable/entrée dish, a sauce boat, a soup tureen

Procedures
to carve, flambé, fillet

Praising food (for comprehension)
delicious, excellent, out of this world, tasty, juicy, fresh, a tender steak, sweet cherries,
I'm enjoying this steak

Criticizing food (for comprehension)
awful, horrible, ghastly, revolting, terrible, tasteless, dry, stale, old, off, tough, sour,
bitter; too hot/sweet, not hot/sweet enough; undercooked, underdone; overcooked,
overdone

Accompaniments
ketchup, mustard, gravy, horseradish sauce, mayonnaise, salad dressing, sauce tartare, cream, croutons (*plural*), crackers (*plural*)

Questions to ask during a meal
Is everything all right, Sir/Madam?
Would you like anything/some ketchup/a roll to go with your ...?
Would you like some more wine/another roll?

Responding to requests
Certainly, Sir/Madam. I'll bring you some .../a ... straightaway. I'll get you some .../a ... straightaway.
I'm very sorry, Sir/Madam. We have none./We don't have any./We don't have that./We have no ... Perhaps you'd like some .../a ... instead?

Customers' wishes (for comprehension)
No, thanks. I won't have any. I'd better not.
I don't want much/many; Not too much/many.
Please. Yes, please.
(Just) a little/a few; (just) a couple; a tiny slice/portion/helping; go easy with the ..., lots, a lot; plenty, a large/good-sized helping.

Later stages of the meal

To start you off

1 Think of a good restaurant that you know. Which of these items would it serve after the main course? Would it serve any other items which are not on the list? In what order would it serve the items?

(a) petits fours, mints, Turkish delight, or other small sweets
(b) cheese
(c) coffee
(d) dessert
(e) cigars
(f) liqueurs
(g) fresh fruit
(h) dessert wine or fortified wine

2 The table sets out some of the basic ingredients and prepared elements of desserts. From the list on page 75, can you find two more items for each heading?

Fruits	Nuts	Dried fruits	Other basic ingredients
oranges	walnuts	currants	flour

Flavourings	Prepared elements
coffee	meringue

almonds – batter – cherries – cinnamon – cream – eggs – ginger – pastry – pineapple – pistachios – plums – raisins – prunes – vanilla

How many more items of each type can you name? (You will find lists of these items on page 81 and pages 154–173.)

3   Which verb goes with which picture?

to beat – to chop – to dip – to grate – to grind (*past tense:* ground) – to shred – to whip

4   Can you name desserts of these different kinds?

(a) very sweet – not very sweet – rich – light – not fattening
(b) which contain no flour
(c) which contain no or very little sugar

5   Can you name desserts which include:

jelly – ice cream – whipped cream – short pastry – flaky pastry – choux pastry – sponge (cake) – chocolate – marzipan

6 Add any cheeses that you know to this list:

Strong: Gorgonzola
Rather strong: Cheddar
Mild: Philadelphia
Rather mild: Brie
Hard: Cheddar
Medium hard: Gorgonzola
Soft: Brie
Cream: Philadelphia
Blue: Gorgonzola

You will use the list in Exercises 13 and 14.

Developing the topic

7 You will hear a list of fifteen ingredients that can be used in desserts. Write down each ingredient. For example:

1. *sliced oranges*

Play the tape again, and follow the procedure for Exercise 7 on page 4.

8 Listen to the descriptions of three desserts, and complete the details in the chart.

	Apple Charlotte	Apricot amber	Malakoff pudding
It's a	cold _____.	_____ _____ _____	_____ _____.
It consists of	cooked, _____ apples, _____ crumbs and _____ of _____.	_____ and _____ _____ _____ in _____	a mixture of _____, _____ _____, _____ _____ and _____
with	—	_____ _____ _____ on top.	_____ _____ _____.
It's flavoured with	_____	—	_____.
and it's served with	_____ _____.	—	—

9 Play the tape again, and follow the procedure for Exercise 7 on page 4.

10 Work on your own or with a partner. Use the framework in Exercise 8 to write explanations of three desserts. Then read your explanations to another student or group of students. They should try to guess what dessert you are explaining. Together discuss the wording of your explanations: if they are accurate, if there is enough information, and so on.

11 Use the framework below to compare desserts from the menu on page 44, like this: *The chocolate brandy cake is richer than the cream caramel.*

The	chocolate brandy cake cherry and almond tart cream caramel fresh fruit salad	is	sweeter richer lighter		than the	. . .
			contains more	cream sugar		
		is less	sweet rich			
		contains less		cream sugar		

12 Write down a list of six desserts for a menu, and compare them in the same way.

13 Use the information in the list in Exercise 6 to describe various cheeses. For example:

Brie is a rather mild, soft cheese.
Cheddar is a rather strong, hard cheese.
Gorgonzola is a strong, medium hard, blue cheese.

14   Use the information from Exercise 6. Take turns to be A (a customer) or B (a waiter/waitress).

A

Which is	stronger: milder: harder: softer:	the ... or the ...?

B

Oh, the	...	is stronger etc.	than the ...

15   Find the right description in column 2 for each kind of coffee in column 1. For example: *(a)* = *5.*

(a) black
(b) white
(c) capuccino
(d) espresso
(e) decaffeinated/ decaf/Hag
(f) Irish
(g) Caribbean
(h) Turkish

1. strong coffee combined with hot milk, with ground cinammon and nutmeg on top
2. coffee with no caffeine in it
3. strong black coffee, boiled with sugar
4. strong coffee with Irish whisky, brown sugar and cream
5. coffee without milk or cream
6. strong black coffee, made by forcing steam through the coffee
7. coffee with milk or cream
8. strong coffee with rum, brown sugar and cream

In the same way, describe any other kinds of coffee which are usual in your region.

[cassette icon]

16 You will hear three orders for coffee. Note down the orders, putting a tick in columns 4, 5 or 6.

Order No.	Types of coffee	Details	Before next course	With next course	After next course
1	2 black 1 ...	with ...	✓		
2					
3					

[cassette icon]

17 You will hear a waiter taking down two customers' orders for the later stages of a meal. Write down the order. First, the waiter wants to know if the woman has finished her meat course.

Woman	Man
1. 2. 3.	1. 2. 3.

[cassette icon]

18 Study and then practise the waiter's sentences. Follow the procedure for Exercise 7 on page 4.

Follow-up

19   Work with a partner who knows your language. Take turns to be A or B. A should say the names of dessert ingredients in your language; B should say the names in English, as quickly as possible. For example:

A: *mantequilla fundida*.   B: *melted butter*.
A: *crème*.   B: *cream*.

20   Work with one or more students. Write down the names of three suitable desserts for each of these types of customer:

(a) diabetic
(b) on a low-fat diet
(c) Jewish, having had meat for the main course
(d) with ulcers
(e) loves really sweet desserts
(f) wants something light

You will use these lists in Exercise 21.

21   Work with a partner. Using the lists you drew up in Exercise 20, take turns to be A (a customer) and B (a waiter/waitress). B should answer A's questions.

A	**B**
I'm diabetic/I have ulcers, etc. What could I have?	I'd suggest the . . .
Which is sweeter/etc.? Which contains less sugar/etc.?	The . . . is sweeter/etc. than the . . . The . . . contains less sugar/etc. than the . . .

22   Rôle-play in groups. Draw up a menu for the later stages of a meal, or use an existing menu. Practise giving and taking orders for desserts, cheese, coffee and liqueurs. Include customers who ask for explanations or advice.

Language reference

Types of desserts/sweets
a cake, a mousse, a pudding, a pie (= with pastry on top, Brit.E; with or without pastry on top, Am.E), a tart (= without pastry on top, Brit.E)

Ingredients in desserts (see pages 154–173 for more detailed lists)
Fruits (*countable*): apples, apricots, cherries, oranges, peaches, pears, plums
Nuts (*countable*): almonds, pistachios, walnuts
(*uncountable*): coconut
Dried fruit (*countable*): currants, raisins, sultanas
(*uncountable*): mixed dried fruit
Other basic ingredients (*countable*): eggs, egg whites, egg yolks
(*uncountable*): butter, chocolate, cream, flour, milk, sugar
Flavourings (*uncountable*): cinnamon, coffee, chocolate, ginger, nutmeg, rum, vanilla
Prepared elements (*uncountable*): batter, ice cream, jam, jelly, meringue, choux pastry, flaky pastry, short pastry

Preparation of ingredients
Chopped nuts, **ground** almonds, **grated** nutmeg, **shredded** coconut, **sliced** apples, **mixed dried** fruit, **whipped** cream, **beaten** eggs/egg whites, **tinned** peaches, apples **dipped** in batter, **stewed** fruit

Describing desserts/sweets
cold, hot, sweet, rich, fattening, heavy, light; contains (no) sugar/flour

Describing fruit
raw, fresh, dried, cooked, baked, poached, stewed

Describing cheeses
strong, (rather) mild, (medium) hard, (medium) soft, blue, cream

Types of coffee
black, white with cream/milk, cappucino, espresso, Irish, Caribbean, Turkish, decaffeinated/decaf/Hag

Compound nouns
apricot sauce, fruit pie

Comparing
The Gorgonzola is **stronger than** the Brie.
The chocolate cake contains **more sugar than** the fruit salad.
The fruit salad is **less rich and** contains **less sugar than** the chocolate cake.

Polite questions
Will that be sufficient, Sir/Madam? (Have you finished? *Informal*)
Would you like dessert?

Drinks

To start you off

1 List each of the following drinks against its correct heading in the list below. For example: *Spirits : vodka,* ...

ginger ale/beer – Perrier – Cointreau – Dubonnet – vodka – Tabasco – Crème de menthe – whisky – lemonade – Evian – tomato juice – Campari – Grand Marnier – vermouth – Vittel – Angostura bitters – orange squash – Bénédictine – sherry

Add to the lists any drinks which are usual in your region.

Spirits:
Other apéritifs:
Liqueurs:
Mineral water:
Other non-alcoholic/soft drinks:
Mixes:

2 Look at the list of drinks below. Can you say what the usual combinations are? For example: *gin and orange (juice), gin and bitter lemon, gin and* ...

whisky	soda
gin	bitter lemon
Bourbon	tomato juice
vodka	Coke
brandy	tonic water
rum	ginger
	lime
	water

3   In the second column, find and complete the opposites of the drinks in the first column. For example: *a short drink* — *a long drink*. You will use your answers in Exercise 5.

a short drink	... bottled ...
a single whisky	... sparkling/carbonated/fizzy★ ...
a light beer	... soft/non-alcoholic ...
some still mineral water	... sweet ...
a dry sherry or vermouth	... long ...
a draught beer	... double ...
an alcoholic drink	... and soda or water
a neat (Am.E = straight) whisky	... strong ...

(*★Informal*)

4   When customers ask for drinks, they may use the phrases in the first column. Find and complete the correct explanations in the second column. You will hear some of the phrases in Exercise 5.

On the rocks.	I want only a little ...
Thank you!	With ice, and nothing else.
A stiff whisky.	Stop pouring now.
Go easy on the soda.	A large ... with nothing added.

Developing the topic

5   You will hear five customers ordering drinks. Listen once and put ticks (√) to indicate each customer's order. Then listen again, and indicate if the customer wants only a little (+) or a lot (+ +).

	1	2	3	4	5
whisky					
brandy					
gin	✓ ++				
vodka					
soda					
tonic	✓ +				
orange juice					
ice					

[cassette icon]

6 Study and then practise the waiters' sentences. Follow the procedure for Exercise 7 on page 4.

7 Work with a partner. Take turns to be A, a customer, and B, a waiter/waitress who is making suggestions. Use language from Exercises 1 and 2, and include other drinks that are usual in your region.

A   **B**

I'd like	something non-alcoholic. a long cool drink. an apéritif. a liqueur. a soft drink. some mineral water.	Certainly, Sir/Madam.	
		How about	a gin and tonic? a Dubonnet? etc.

8   Work with a partner. Take turns to be A, a customer, and B, a waiter/waitress. Use language from Exercise 3. B should reply sometimes as in (i) and sometimes as in (ii).

A

I'd like I think I'll have Can you get me	a	whisky/Scotch gin beer
	some	mineral water

B

A whisky (etc.), Sir/Madam?
(i) Single or double?   ... or ...?
(ii) Would you like some tonic/soda (etc.) with that?

9   You will hear three customers ordering several drinks each. They speak at natural speed and so you may need to listen more than once. First, listen and put ticks (√) to show how many drinks each customer wants. Then listen again and write the name of the drink under each tick.

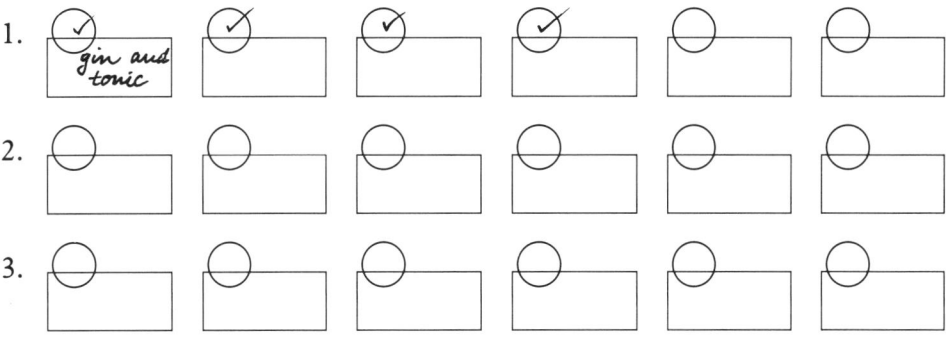

10   Study and practise the waiters' sentences. Follow the procedure for Exercise 7 on page 4.

Follow-up

11   Work in pairs. Write down the names of sixteen alcoholic and non-alcoholic drinks, each on a separate slip of paper. Put the slips of paper in a box or large envelope. Take turns to be A (waiter/waitress) and B (a customer). B should pull out four slips, and prepare to order the four drinks, giving student A all the necessary information. For example: *Can you get us one double Scotch on the rocks, a soda with ice, a small medium dry sherry and a tomato juice without ice?* Student A should repeat the order and write it down, then check with B that he or she has written it down correctly.

12   Work in the same way, but this time B should give some incomplete orders; for example: *Can you get us a Scotch?* and Student A should ask for further information; for example: *A Scotch? Certainly, Sir. A single or double? Would you like it on the rocks?* etc.

Language reference

General categories of drinks
spirits, apéritifs, liqueurs, mineral water, non-alcoholic/soft drinks, mixes (for wines, see Unit 6)

Spirits
bourbon, brandy, gin, rum, rye (whisky), Scotch (whisky), vodka

Apéritifs
Campari, Dubonnet, sherry

Liqueurs
Bénédictine, Cointreau, crème de menthe, Grand Marnier

Mineral water
Evian, Perrier, Vittel

Non-alcoholic/soft drinks
bitter lemon, Coca-Cola, ginger (beer/ale), lemonade, (orange) juice, (orange) squash, soda (water), tomato juice, tonic (water)

Mixes
Angostura bitters, Tabasco, Worcester sauce

Garnishes
maraschino cherry, lemon slice, sprig of mint, olive

Describing drinks
long, short; large, small; alcoholic, soft/non-alcoholic; still, sparkling/carbonated/fizzy (*informal*); draught, bottled beer; light, strong beer; dry, sweet sherry; single, double whisky; neat (Am.E = straight); a stiff (brandy); with/without ice/lemon; on the rocks

Description of quantity *(for comprehension)*
a little, a splash, a dash, a spot; go easy on the water; don't drown it! Thank you!/Thanks! (= Stop pouring!) plenty of soda; fill it up!

Making suggestions
How about a sherry?

Asking what a customer wants
What can I get you, Sir/Madam?
Would would you like, Sir/Madam?

Stating the price
That'll be $5.60, Sir/Madam.

Talking about money

To start you off

1 On the left are phrases which one may find on a menu. On the right are the explanations which a head waiter might give to a customer who is paying a bill. Find the explanations to match the phrases. For example: *(a) = 3.*

(a) *There is no service charge. Gratuities are at your discretion.*

> 1. Yes, Madam. You can use your American Express card.

(b) **All major credit cards accepted.**

> 2. The cost of your meal is $65, Sir. The extra $6.50 is for the waiter.

(c) We regret we do not accept credit cards.

> 3. The bill doesn't include service, Sir. If you would like to give the waitress something, that's for you to decide.

(d) **ALL PRICES INCLUDE ... TAX.**

> 4. We have to add this amount for . . . tax, Madam. It's 8% of the cost of the meal.

(e) *Cover charge: $2.00.*

> 5. This isn't for any food or drink, Madam. We add this sum to every bill, for the rolls, linen, and so on.

(f) 10% SERVICE CHARGE WILL BE ADDED.

> 6. You don't pay anything extra for . . . tax, Sir. It's already in the price of the meal.

(g) **All prices are exclusive of . . . tax at the current rate.**

> 7. I'm very sorry, Sir; you won't be able to use your Diner's Club card. Could you pay in cash or by traveller's cheque?

2 Write down these numbers and symbols in words. You will hear them in Exercise 3.

(a) 12; 14; 40; 52; 137; 286; 1,473.
(b) $5+13$; $22-4$; 8×11; $45\div9$.
(c) 10.5; 15%; $193-10\%$; $16.50.

Developing the topic

3 Listen and check your answers to sections (a), (b) and (c) in Exercise 2. Then write down in numbers the phrases that you hear in section (d).

4 Play the tape again, and practise saying the numbers.

5 Use the table below to express the seven pieces of information in Exercise 1; for example: *1. American Express cards are accepted.*

1. American Express cards	is	(not)	accepted
2. A 10% service charge	are		included in the bill
3. A service charge			added to the bill
4. 8% hospital tax			
5. A $2.00 cover charge			
6. 8% Value Added Tax			
7. Credit cards			

6 You will hear six customers asking about paying their bills. First, make sure you know what the words below mean. Then listen and tick (√) the right box for each customer to show what he or she is asking about. Add any details in the last column.

	Cash (local currency)	Foreign currency	Traveller's cheques	Credit card	Cheque plus banker's card	Details
1.		✓				US dollars
2.						
3.						
4.						
5.						
6.						

7 Listen again and practise the waiter's replies. Follow the procedure for Exercise 7 on page 4.

8 Work with a partner. Take turns to be A (a waiter/waitress) and B (a customer, who is ready to pay the bill). Use phrases from Exercise 6.

A	How will you be paying, Sir/Madam?		
B	In	cash. US dollars/French francs/etc.	OK? All right?
	By	credit card. traveller's cheque. cheque with a banker's card.	
A	(i)	That'll be fine, Sir/Madam.	
	(ii)	I'm very sorry, Sir/Madam. We don't accept … We only accept …	
	(iii)	I'll just ask the manager/cashier/… about that.	

9 Work in the same way. This time, after B has said how he/she wants to pay, continue:

A	By which card? In which currency? May I see your card?	**B** (*Answers or shows card*)
A	(i) That'll be fine, Sir/Madam. Could you please sign here. Could you please make out your cheque to Restaurant Chez Nous …	
	(ii) I'm very sorry …, (iii) I'll just ask … (*As in Exercise 8*)	
	(iv) I'm sorry, Sir/Madam. This card has expired.	

```
                                              047045

                        ❖
              RESTAURANT FRANÇAIS
            CHEZ NOUS

      | Table    6 | Persons    1 | Date  21/7 |

   1 _____  Cover              1.20
   2 _____  Beer               1.50
   3 _____  Starter            2.50
   4 _____  R. Chicken         4.85
   5 _____  Potatoes (sauté)   1.00
   6 _____  Fr. beans          1.00
   7 _____  Beer               1.50
   8 _____  Dessert            2.00
   9 _____  Cig                1.50
  10 _____
  11 _____
  12 _____
  13 _____
  14 _____
  15 _____
                         Total  17.05
                         %    _____
                       ----------------
```

10   A customer and a waiter are talking about this bill. Try to complete the missing words. You will hear them in Exercise 11.

(a) WAITER: Item 1 is the c - - - - ch - - - -.

(b) CUSTOMER: The vegetables weren't in - - - - - -?
    WAITER: No, Sir. They were ex - - -.

(c) CUSTOMER: You seem to have ch - - -ed me twice for the dessert.
    WAITER: I'll just go and ch - - - it for you, Sir.

11   Listen and check your answers to Exercise 10. Then practise the waiter's replies. Follow the procedure for Exercise 7 on page 4.

Follow-up

12   Work with a partner. Take turns to be A or B. A holds up figures etc. as in Exercise 3. B says them in English.

13   Look at some menus and explain the prices in them. For example:
The French fries are included in this price.
A 15% service charge is added to the bill.

14   Work with a partner. Make up some bills. Take turns to be A (a waiter/waitress) and B (a customer). Practise the conversation between them, from the moment when B asks for the bill until he or she gets the receipt.

Language reference

Figures and sums
Cardinal numbers (1 − several thousand): plus, minus/less, multiplied by/times, divided by; point; per cent

Money
a bill, a receipt, (local) currency, change

Items on a bill
cover/a cover charge, tax, service/a service charge, a gratuity

Compound nouns
Sales Tax, hospital tax, Value Added Tax

Ways of paying
in cash, in (foreign) currency, in (dollars) etc; by credit card, by traveller's cheque, by cheque with a banker's card

Explaining a bill
Hospital Tax **is added to** the bill.
Service **is included in** the bill.
Potatoes are **extra**.

Questions about paying
How will you be paying?
By which card?
In which currency?
May I see your card?

Statements about paying
I'm very sorry, we don't accept credit cards.
We only accept traveller's cheques in dollars.
I'm sorry, Sir/Madam. This card has expired.
I'll just ask the manager about that.
I'll just go and check it for you.

Requests about paying
Could you sign here, please?
Could you please make out your cheque to Chez Nous?

UNIT 12

Complaints and other problems

To start you off

1A If a customer complains, what should a waiter/waitress say or do? Tick (√) the actions which would be correct, and put a cross (×) by those which would be incorrect.

☐ 1. Apologise to the customer.
☐ 2. Be polite and calm.
☐ 3. Listen carefully to the customer.
☐ 4. Ask questions to find out more about the problem if necessary.
☐ 5. Tell the customer that he or she is wrong.
☐ 6. Explain the restaurant's problems in detail.
☐ 7. Talk more loudly than the customer.
☐ 8. Take prompt action.
☐ 9. Suggest that the customer is complaining about something that is not very important.
☐ 10. Call a senior member of staff (e.g. Head Waiter), if you feel that you cannot deal with the problem.
☐ 11. Tell the customer what you are going to do.
☐ 12. Maintain the customer's confidence in the restaurant.
☐ 13. Say nothing and continue serving.
☐ 14. Thank the customer for bringing the matter to your attention.

1B If the customer praises the food or service what should a waiter/waitress say or do?

☐ 1. Smile and thank the customer.
☐ 2. Say nothing.

☐   3. React with embarrassment.
☐   4. Ask for a larger tip.
☐   5. Say 'That's very kind of you'.
☐   6. Tell the customer you will pass on the compliment to other staff (as appropriate).
☐   7. Ask the customer to write a letter to the manager.
☐   8. Say 'I'm glad you like it'.
☐   9. Say 'Of course!' and laugh.

2   Make lists of things about which customers may complain, under these headings.

The food: for example, *cold*
The service: for example, *slow*
Equipment: for example, *dirty cutlery*
The environment: for example, *air conditioning too cold*
Accident: for example, *wine spilt on guest's jacket*

3   What action should restaurant staff take if:

(a) The food or drink is spilt on guest's clothing?
(b) A guest becomes ill?
(c) The wrong dish is served.
(d) The food was not served as ordered by the customer.
(e) The wine was bad.
(f) The waiter forgot to serve a dish.

4   Make a list (in your own language, if you like) of problems which customers may create for restaurant staff. For example: *A customer arrives in a swimsuit.* Compare your list with other students' lists. You will use your list in Exercise 12.

Developing the topic

5   You will hear six customers complaining. Listen once, and make a note of each problem. For example: *1. Too cold by the window.*

Then draw up four columns, as below, listen again, and write down the staff's actual words for customers 2–6 in each column. You will use some of these words in Exercise 11.

	Apology	Excuse	Offer of action	Maintaining customer confidence
1.	I'm sorry, Sir.	- -	I'll ask the Head Waiter about another table.	I'm sure we can find you something more suitable.
2.	I'm ...	There must be some mistake.		We'll make sure ...
3.				
4.				
5.				
6.				

6 Play the tape again. Study and practise the staff's words. Follow the procedure for Exercise 7, page 4.

7A Sometimes staff have to tell customers about a restaurant regulation. Use the

language below to explain each regulation. For example: *I'm very sorry, Madam.*
Ladies may not wear casual trousers in the restaurant.

Gentleman Ladies Guests	have to may not	wear play bring smoke	jackets and ties casual trousers transistors dogs long sleeves	in the restaurant in this part of the restaurant into the restaurant

You will use these explanations in Exercise 8.

7B Sometimes staff can make helpful suggestions. Use the table below to make
suggestions to the customers in the pictures. Perhaps you can add some suggestions
of your own.

Perhaps you	would like to could	borrow a tie. borrow a jacket. eat in the coffee shop instead. leave your dog in your car. . . .
We	could	lend you a tie. put your dog in . . . . . .

8 Work with a partner. Take turns to be A (a waiter/waitress) and B (a customer). Use the table below to act out the situations in the pictures in Exercise 7.

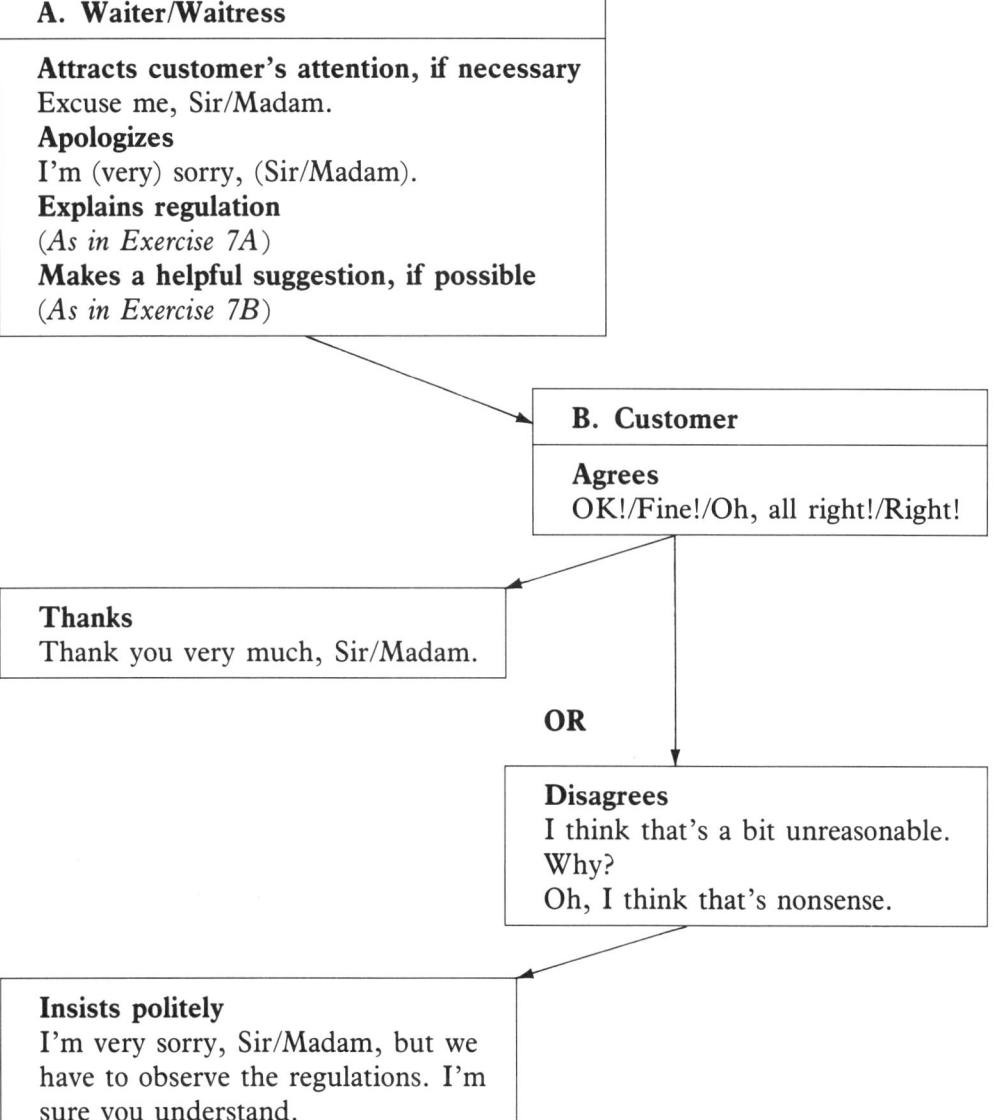

A. Waiter/Waitress

Attracts customer's attention, if necessary
Excuse me, Sir/Madam.
Apologizes
I'm (very) sorry, (Sir/Madam).
Explains regulation
(*As in Exercise 7A*)
Makes a helpful suggestion, if possible
(*As in Exercise 7B*)

B. Customer

Agrees
OK!/Fine!/Oh, all right!/Right!

Thanks
Thank you very much, Sir/Madam.

OR

Disagrees
I think that's a bit unreasonable.
Why?
Oh, I think that's nonsense.

Insists politely
I'm very sorry, Sir/Madam, but we
have to observe the regulations. I'm
sure you understand.

Follow-up

9   Make a list of five things about which a customer might complain in a restaurant. Work with a partner. Take turns to be A (a waiter/waitress) and B (a customer). B should complain about one of the things on his/her list. A should respond by using and adapting the language in Exercise 5. Continue with the other complaints on your list.

10   In Exercise 4 you made a list of problems which customers may create in a restaurant. Use your list and work with a partner. B (the customer) should simply state the problem. Then A (the waiter/waitress) and B should continue the conversation, using and adapting language from Exercises 7 and 8.

Language reference (See also Unit 4 for complaints about equipment, and Unit 8 for complaints about food.)

Apologising
I'm sorry (*for a small problem; for example, if there is no ash tray on the table*).
I'm so sorry/I'm very sorry (*for more serious problem; for example, if some food is not fresh*).
I'm extremely sorry (*for a really serious problem; for example, if the waiter has spilt some food on a customer's clothing*).

Asking about problems
What seems to be the problem, Sir/Madam? (*formal*)
What's the problem, Sir/Madam?
Is there a problem, Sir/Madam?

Making excuses
There must be some mistake. (= I am sure there is a mistake.)

Maintaining the customer's confidence
I'll/We'll (try to) make sure you enjoy your meal.
I think/hope you'll enjoy/like ......

Offers of action
I'll change it for you immediately.
I'll ask the Head Waiter about that.
Would you like to order something else?
We'll be happy to pay the cleaning bill.
Shall I have the chef heat this up for you?

Attracting a customer's attention
Excuse me, Sir/Madam.

Polite refusals
I'm afraid (= I regret) that won't be possible.

Expressing sympathy
I understand how you feel, Sir/Madam.

Explaining regulations with *have to* and *may not*
Gentleman *have to* wear jackets and ties.
Ladies *may not* wear casual trousers.

Suggesting other courses of action
Perhaps you would like to borrow a tie?
Perhaps you could leave your dog in your car?
We could lend you a jacket.

Insisting about regulations
We have to observe the regulations.

UNIT 13

Banqueting arrangements

To start you off

1 Many restaurants have banqueting facilities: they can arrange meals in a special dining room for functions such as weddings, company dinners, or press conferences. What kinds of private and public functions are usual in restaurants in your area? List them. For example:

Private
Weddings
Birthday parties
Dinner dances

Public
Company dinners
Press conferences
Fashion shows

For which of these functions is table service usual, and for which of them is buffet service usual? (For some functions, of course, both kinds of service may be appropriate.)

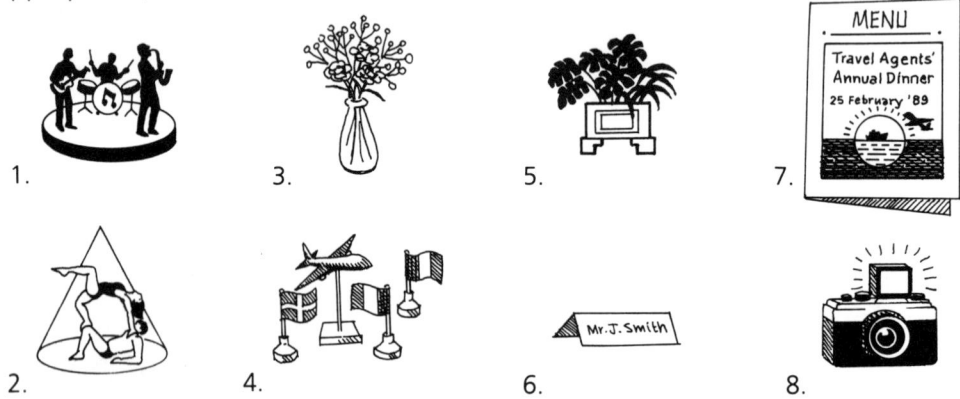

1.

2.

3.

4.

5.

6.

7.

8.

2 A restaurant may provide these things for its banqueting customers. Look at the pictures and fill in the crossword from the clues.

Clues

1. A _____
2. A _____
3. _____
4. Special table _____
5. _____
6. Place _____
7. A special menu _____
8. A _____

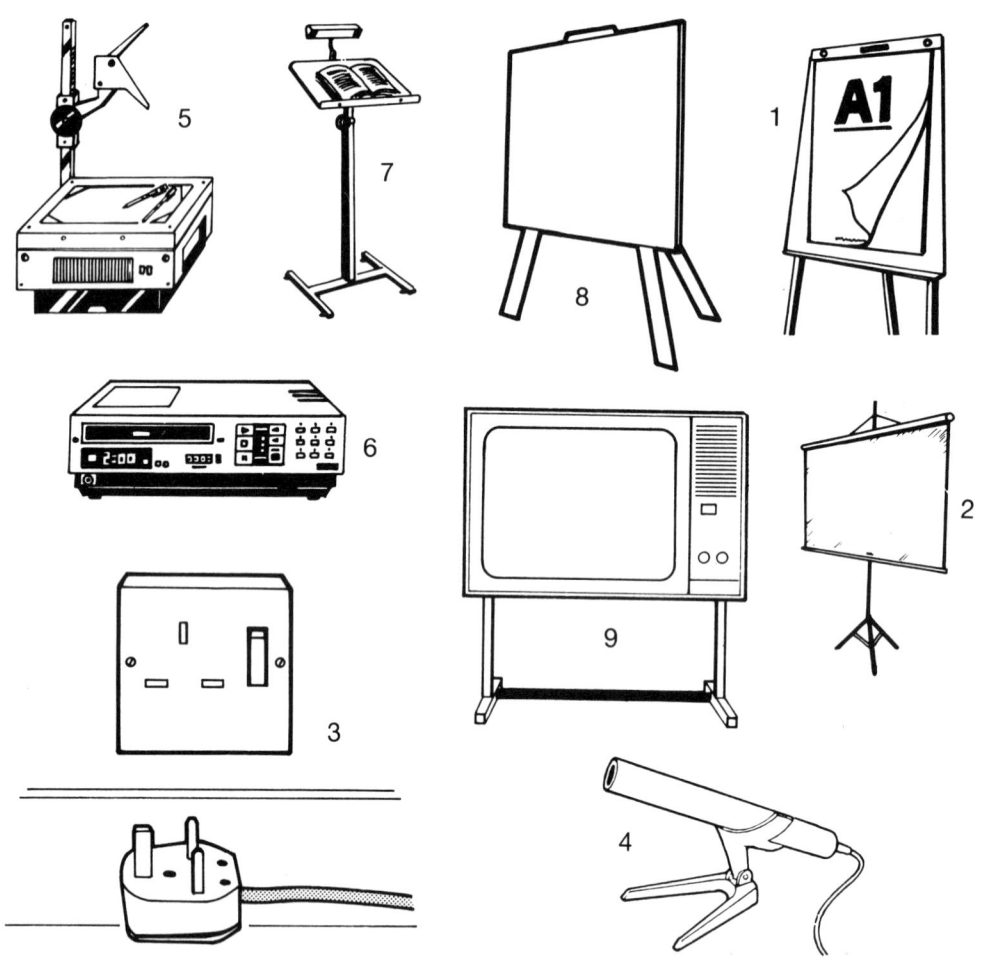

3 Match up the names with the pictures. Put the number in the box. For example:

Blackboard and easel $\boxed{8}$
Microphone $\boxed{}$
Film screen $\boxed{}$
Lectern $\boxed{}$
Overhead projector $\boxed{}$
Flip chart and stand $\boxed{}$
Television $\boxed{}$
Video recorder $\boxed{}$
Electric point $\boxed{}$

4   When a banqueting manager begins discussing arrangements with a customer, he or she needs to obtain the information which is listed below. Do you remember how to ask these kinds of questions politely? (See Exercise 9, page 20, in Unit 3.) Write down the questions you would ask. You will hear them in Exercise 5.

Date: For what day w - - - - that be?
Time: W - - - - th - - b - for lunch or d - - - - -?
Type of Function: Wh - - s - - - of function - - it?
Number of people: How - - - - people - - - - - there - - ?
Price per head: How - - - - per head - - - - - you - - - - to spend?
Wines: included or charged: W - - - - that in - - - - - wines, or w - - - - they be ex - - -?

Developing the topic

5   Listen as a banqueting manager receives a phone call from a customer. First, check your answers to Exercise 4. Then listen again, and note down the information which the customer gives to the five questions above.

6   Play the tape again. Practise the banqueting manager's sentences. Follow the procedure for Exercise 7, page 4.

7   On the next page is the letter from the Forest Hotel Banqueting Manager to Mr Richardson. Put in the missing words:

approximately	includes
charged	information
confirm	reception
enclose	success
forward	telephone

Forest Hotel

Mr James Richardson   4 January 1989
International Consultants Ltd
130 Gloucester Avenue
London NW1 7EG

Dear Mr Richardson,

Thank you for your *telephone* call of 3 January. I would like to _____
the reservation of our Fountain Room for your _____ on Wednesday, 1st
February for _____ twenty guests.

I _____ our Banqueting Information Pack, which _____ our menus and
wine lists. Drinks would be _____ extra at our standard prices.

Please let me know if you would like any further _____.

I look _____ to hearing from you. We will naturally do our best to
make your reception a _____.

Yours sincerely,

Tessa Williams.

Tessa Williams
Banqueting Manager

8 A banqueting manager may need to describe reception rooms to customers.

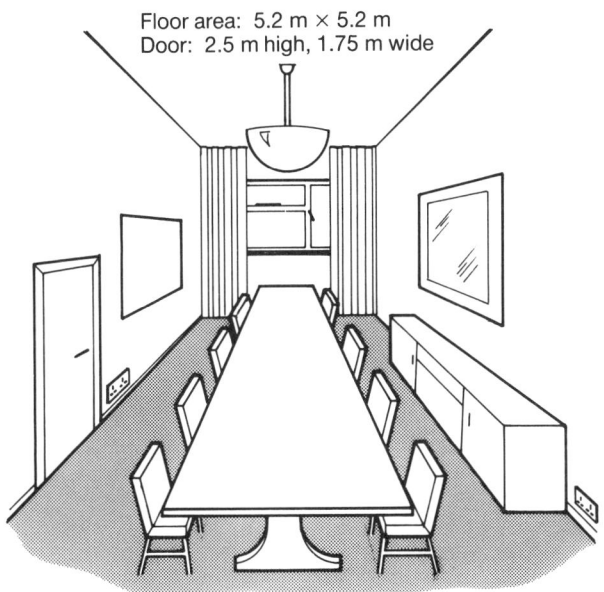

Floor area: 5.2 m × 5.2 m
Door: 2.5 m high, 1.75 m wide

Possible questions about a room	Information about a room
What size is the room? How big/large is the room?	The room is approximately 5 metres square/25 square metres. It measures approximately 5 metres by 5 metres.
How high is the door? What is the height of the door?	The door is $2\frac{1}{2}$ m high.
How wide is the door? What is the width of the door?	It is $1\frac{3}{4}$ m wide.
What sort of floor has the room got?	The room is carpeted. The room has a wooden/tiled/etc. floor.

Possible questions about a room	Information about a room
How is it furnished? What furniture does it contain?	It is furnished with chairs and one large table.
How is it equipped? What equipment does it contain?	It is equipped with a blackboard and two electric points. It can also be equipped with microphones, a video recorder etc.
What do you charge for microphones? How much would the video recorder be?	There would be no charge for microphones. The charge for the video recorder would be £10.00 per day.

Work with a partner. Take turns to be A or B. B should think of a room in your college or establishment. A should ask B some of the questions in column 1 above, and try to guess what room B is thinking of. A can ask the questions in any order.

9
(a) Study the information opposite about conference and banqueting facilities.
(b) Listen to three customers asking questions and receiving answers about facilities.
(c) Listen to the next five questions. When you hear the tone, stop the tape and answer the questions yourself.

10 Work with a partner. For Student A's part, see below. For Student B's part, see page 152 in Appendix 2. You are discussing the details of some banqueting arrangements.

Student A

(a) You are a banqueting manager, and Student B is John or Jane Long, the Sales Manager of International Hire-a-Car Inc. Ask these questions, and note B's answers. You will use your notes in Exercise 11.

1. What sort of service would you like?
2. What sort of table plan would you like?
3. Would you like place cards?
4. What about music?

Conference and Banqueting Facilities

The Statesman Suite is an ideal setting for any type of function. This modern and elegant area is located on the first floor and has a bright glass verandah overlooking the forest. The suite can be divided with acoustic folding partitions to provide the right ambience for any number from 12 to 200 persons depending on the type of function or table setting requirements. Its quiet location is an ideal venue for meetings, conferences, training courses and private parties.

Three Conference Rooms are available in addition to the Statesman Suite.

All these facilities are accessible by lift or stairs.

Statesman I

Theatre style seating	170
Classroom style seating	90
Dinner Dances	160
Wedding Receptions	160

Statesman II and III

Theatre style seating	50
Classroom style seating	30
Dinners	40
Wedding Receptions	40

Conference Rooms

3 Conference rooms available from 9.00 – 5.00

Equipment available:

Blackboard and easel	no charge
Microphones	no charge
1.5 metre screen	£5.00 per day
Lectern	no charge
Overhead projector	£17.50 per day
Flip chart and stand	£5.00 per day
Televisions	£5.00 per day
Video recorder	£10.00 per day

Additional equipment can be hired on request.

5. What sort of table decoration would you like?
6. What sort of design would you like for the menus?
7. Would you like a photographer?
8. Do you have any special wishes as regards food?
9. How will you be paying?

(b) You are John or Janet King, the Marketing Manager of Far Eastern Travel Ltd and you are discussing details for a sales conference banquet with B, a banqueting manager. Answer B's questions. This is what you want:

1. Buffet service.
2. A three-piece band and a cabaret.
3. Yellow and white flowers; decoration of small elephants or tigers on the buffet table.
4. Very attractive menu booklets, also decorated with elephants or tigers.
5. A photographer.
6. There will be three Muslim and five Hindu participants requiring special dishes.
7. The bill should be sent to the Financial Controller of Far Eastern Travel Ltd.

11   Write a letter confirming the arrangements that you made as a banqueting manager in Exercise 10. Begin:

Dear Mr/Ms/Mrs/Miss (*Name*)

I am writing to confirm the details we agreed for your (*function*) on (*date*), as follows:

. . .   (*Give the details.*)

We look forward to making your (*function*) a successful and enjoyable event.

Yours sincerely,

(*Your name*)
Banqueting Manager

Follow-up

12 Work with one or several other students. Take turns to be banqueting staff or customers, discussing the arrangements for a banqueting function.

(a) Decide what the function is (for example, a dinner dance for the staff of a local airline).
(b) The banqueting staff should obtain basic information from the customer, as in Exercise 4.
(c) In pairs or as a group, write the letter of confirmation regarding this information.
(d) Then together plan some of the details as in Exercise 9. Ask and answer questions, and make suggestions. For example:
   How about a cabaret?
   How about arranging the tables in a circle?
(e) In pairs or as a group, write the letter of confirmation regarding these details.

Language reference

Banqueting events
a function; a reception, a wedding, a birthday party, a dinner dance, a company dinner, a press conference, a fashion show

Types of service
table service, buffet service, self-service

Detailed arrangements
the type of function, the table plan, a band, a cabaret, table decorations, place cards, a special menu design, a photographer

Equipment
a flip chart and stand, a blackboard (and easel), a film screen, an electric point (Am.E = outlet), a microphone, an overhead projector, a television (set), a video recorder, a lectern

Expressing the dimensions of a room
The room is (about/approximately/roughly) 5 metres square/25 square metres.
It measures 4 metres by $6\frac{1}{4}$ metres.
The door is $2\frac{1}{2}$ metres high and $1\frac{3}{4}$ metres wide.

Describing a room
It is furnished with tables and chairs.
It is equipped with a blackboard and electric points (Am.E = outlets)
It is carpeted. It has a wooden/tiled/etc. floor.

Explaining charges
£20 per head/per person.
That would include wines.
Drinks would be (charged) extra.
There would be no charge for microphones.
The charge for the video recorder would be £10.00 per day.

Polite questions
Would you like place cards?
What sort of table plan would you like?
What about music? (= Would you like any music?)
How will you be paying?
Do you have any special wishes as regards food?

Suggestions
How about a band?
How about arranging the tables in a circle?

Semi-formal letters *(To a person whose name one knows)*:

Dear Mr/Ms King,

I would like to confirm/This is to confirm . . .
I enclose some information about . . .
The pack includes . . .
Please let me/us know if you would like any further information.
I/We look forward to hearing from you.
I/We will naturally do our best to . . .

Yours sincerely, (Am.E = Yours (very) truly)

Breakfast

To start you off

1 As you know, breakfast menus are very different in different countries. Which of the items below would be usual for breakfast in the following countries?

(a) France, Spain, Portugal or Italy
(b) The United States
(c) Britian
(d) Scandinavia or Holland
(e) Other countries whose nationals often visit your region

Beverages
Orange Juice
Coffee
Tea
Cold milk
Iced Water
Hot Chocolate

Cereals
Muesli
Cornflakes, etc.
Porridge

Fruit
Fresh half grapefruit
Stewed prunes
Chilled melon

Bread, etc.
Bread
Toast
Croissants or rolls
Danish pastries
Waffles or pancakes

Accompaniments
Jam
Marmalade
Honey
Maple Syrup

Protein foods
Eggs (boiled, scrambled, poached or fried)
Cheese
Cold meat and sausage
Grilled or fried bacon or sausages
Grilled or fried kippers

2   Add to the lists any foods or drinks that are usual for breakfast in your region.

Developing the topic

Good Morning!
Breakfast at the May Fair

SERVED FROM 6.00 am UNTIL 12 NOON

The May Fair

*A choice of freshly squeezed orange or grapefruit juice, fresh berries
and cream, followed by scrambled eggs on toast with smoked salmon.
Rolls, croissants or Danish pastries, marmalade, preserves and honey.
A choice of tea, coffee, coffee Hag, hot chocolate or milk. All the
above complemented by half a bottle of Champagne.*   **£21.50**

The English

*A choice of freshly squeezed orange or grapefruit juice. Porridge,
cereals, half grapefruit, melon, fresh fruit salad, yoghurt or stewed
prunes. Your choice of two fresh eggs, any style,with bacon or ham,
sausage and tomato. Rolls, croissants or Danish pastry, marmalade,
preserves and honey. A choice of tea, coffee, coffee Hag, hot
chocolate or milk.*   **£9.70**

The Continental

*A choice of freshly squeezed orange or grapefruit juice, rolls,
croissants or Danish pastries, marmalade, preserves and honey. A
choice of tea, coffee Hag, coffee, hot chocolate or milk.*   **£7.50**

The Health Breakfast (calories approx. 225)

*Freshly squeezed orange juice, half grapefruit, poached egg with
tomato or boiled egg, slices of wholemeal bread, tea, coffee.*   **£8.50**

**For your convenience, place your order on the preceding evening;
please use the door knob menu provided or call Room Service.**

[oo]

3 You will hear three customers ordering breakfast from the May Fair breakfast menu. Write each customer's number in the circle, and complete the orders.

◯ **The May Fair Breakfast**

    Juice: _____

    Beverage: _____

◯ **Health Breakfast**

    Egg: _____

    _____ minutes

    Beverage: _____

①**Continental Breakfast**

    Juice: *orange*

    Beverage: _____

[oo]

4 Play the tape again. Practise the waitress's part. Follow the procedure for Exercise 7 on page 4.

5 Here are some questions a waiter/waitress might need to ask when serving breakfast at the May Fair. Put a tick (√) to indicate the breakfast menus to which the questions apply.

	MAYFAIR	ENGLISH	CONTINENTAL	HEALTH
(a) Which juice would you like, orange or grapefruit?	✓	✓	✓	
(b) Would you like cereal, or fruit, or yoghourt?				
(c) Which cereal would you like?				
(d) Which fruit would you like?				
(e) How would you like your egg done?				
(f) How many minutes? (*for boiled egg*)				
(g) Would you like rolls, croissants or Danish pastry?				
(h) What would you like to drink?				

6 You will hear a customer ordering an English breakfast. Tick the items which the customer orders.

THE MAY FAIR

AN INTER·CONTINENTAL HOTEL

LONDON

ENGLISH BREAKFAST

☐ ORANGE JUICE   ☐ GRAPEFRUIT JUICE

With a choice of one of the following items:

☐ RICE KRISPIES   ☐ WEETABIX
☐ ALL BRAN   ☐ CORNFLAKES
☐ PORRIDGE   ☐ PRUNES   ☐ HALF GRAPEFRUIT
☐ YOGHURT   ☐ MELON   ☐ FRESH FRUIT SALAD

EGGS: ☐ FRIED   ☐ POACHED
☐ SCRAMBLED   ☐ BOILED .... MINS
SERVED WITH:
☐ BACON   ☐ SAUSAGE   ☐ TOMATO   ☐ HAM

☐ TEA   ☐ COFFEE   ☐ DE-CAFFEINATED
☐ HOT CHOCOLATE   ☐ MILK

The above served with Toast, Croissants, Rolls, Butter, Preserves and ☐ Danish Pastry.

7 Play the tape again and practise the waitress's part. Follow the procedure for Exercise 7 on page 4.

QO

8 Now you are the waiter/waitress taking an order. Look at the check list in Exercise 6. Stop the tape each time after the customer has spoken, and speak to him.

CUSTOMER: Good morning!
YOU: _____
CUSTOMER: Yes, I am. I'll have orange juice, please.
YOU: _____
CUSTOMER: I don't think I want any cereal. I'll have one of your fruit dishes. Let me see. What have you got?
YOU: _____
CUSTOMER: Right, I'll have the fruit salad. Then I'll have boiled eggs.
YOU: _____
CUSTOMER: Three minutes, please.
YOU: _____
CUSTOMER: Oh, nothing thanks. I'll have them on their own. And what drinks do you have?
YOU: _____
CUSTOMER: OK. I'll have decaffeinated coffee. Right! Thanks very much.

Follow-up

9 Use the May Fair breakfast menu, or a local breakfast menu, or create your own menu. In pairs, take turns to be customers or waiters/waitresses; give and take orders; ask and answer questions as in Exercises 3, 5 and 6.

Language reference

Breakfast foods
Cereals, muesli, cornflakes etc., porridge; toast (*uncountable*), croissants, Danish pastries, waffles, pancakes; jam, marmalade, honey, maple syrup; bacon, kippers, ham, sausages

Ways of cooking eggs
Boiled, poached, scrambled, fried (Am.E = sunny side up)

Questions
Which juice would you like?
How would you like your egg done?
How many minutes?
What would you like your eggs served with?
Would you like rolls or croissants?
What would you like to drink?

Applying for jobs

To start you off

1 Work with one or more students. Make a list of catering establishments which might need personnel who speak English, and the sorts of jobs that they would offer. Use these headings:

Establishment   **Locality**   **Type(s) of job**

2 At a recent conference in London on careers in catering, several employers talked about the personal qualities which they want to find in people who apply for jobs. Which of the listed qualities do you think are necessary for a commis (trainee) waiter/waitress? Which are necessary for a banqueting manager? Which are necessary for both? List the qualities under these headings:

Waiter/waitress	**Banqueting manager**	**Waiter/waitress and banqueting manager**

(a) Very well organised
(b) Good at dealing with different kinds of people
(c) Able to motivate other members of staff
(d) Keen to learn more
(e) Good manners
(f) Really interested in food and its presentation
(g) Imaginative and creative
(h) Enthusiastic about the job
(i) Clean and tidy
(j) Always careful about hygiene
(k) Charming
(l) Tactful

(m) Healthy
(n) Can work as part of a team

Discuss your answers and your reasons for them with other students. You will use your answers in Exercise 14.

3 When you apply for a job, which of these things should you do? Tick (√) the things that you should do. Put a cross (×) by those that you should not do. Discuss your answers, and your reasons for them, with other students.

When you apply
☐ Write a very long letter
☐ Use good quality writing paper
☐ Send a glamorous photo of yourself, if a photo is requested
☐ Send a small passport-type photo if a photo is requested
☐ Send a letter with words crossed out in it
☐ Write very clearly

Before the interview
☐ Find out what you can about the establishment and its activities
☐ Prepare a few questions to ask the interviewer
☐ Dress very glamorously
☐ Dress smartly but quietly
☐ Get letters of reference from relatives

At the interview
☐ Make a lot of critical remarks about your present employer or your college
☐ Ask questions about your responsibilities and duties
☐ Ask questions about salary, tips and fringe benefits

Developing the topic

4 Usually, when you apply for a job, you need to send a curriculum vitae (CV), like the one opposite.

(a) Write out the headings from the form (*Name, Address*, etc.) and fill in the details about yourself. You will use this CV in Exercise 14.
(b) Now, on a separate sheet of paper, add the information you would like to see under these headings five years from now. Discuss your additions with other students.

CURRICULUM VITAE

Name:	James Joseph KING
Address:	40 Alexandra Street London E11 2JE
Telephone:	01-742-5806 (work) 01-988-2673 (home)
Date of birth:	4.8.68
Education:	Beaumont Secondary School, London E11. 1978-84 Waltham Forest College, London E17. 1984-86
Qualifications:	General Certificate of Secondary Education (with Grade C in English and mathematics) City and Guilds Diplomas in cooking skills and waiting skills National Catering Board courses in wines, bar work and food development
Experience:	Waiter/chef de rang at Smithson Hotel, London WC1. 1986 - now. Kitchen porter in restaurants in Paris and Milan. 1985 and 1986 (holiday work).
Interests:	Travelling, reading, learning languages, swimming
References:	The Personnel Manager Smithson Hotel Belsize Avenue London NW3 4PG The Principal Waltham Forest College Forest Road London E17 4JB

PURCELL COURT

Hempton Road, Deddington
Oxfordshire, OX5 4QJ

STATION HEAD WAITER/WAITRESS

Required for luxury country house hotel, situated 12 miles from Oxford.

We are looking for a young person with experience as chef de rang who now wishes to further their career. Position offers excellent career opportunities.

Excellent accommodation and uniform provided. 5-day week. Salary according to experience.

Please write with CV and photograph:
Mr J. Rover, Personnel Manager
Tel: 0869-12583

---

5   James King wrote a letter to apply for this job. Fill in the missing words from the list:

advertised − apply − attended − develop − enclosed − included − offering − application − course − experience − interview − position − Sir − faithfully − forward

---

40 Alexandra Street
London E11 2JE

23 September, 1990

Mr. J.R. Rover
Purcell Court
Hempton Road
Deddington,
Oxford OX5 4QJ

Dear _____ ,
    I am writing to _____ for the _____ of station head waiter in your hotel, which you _____ in the Catering

Journal of 21 September.

As you will see from the _____ curriculum vitae, I have had three years' _____ as a waiter in a three-star London hotel. My work has _____ service in the bar and coffee shop and floor service. I am now chef de rang in the restaurant.

I have also _____ the National Catering Board's courses in wines, bar work and food development.

In addition, I travelled to France and Italy during my college vacations in 1985 and 1986, and worked as a kitchen porter in hotels in Paris and Milan. I am attending an evening _____ in French at the moment.

I would now like to _____ my professional and social skills in a superior establishment, and am therefore very interested in the position you are _____.

If you are interested in my _____, I would be glad to attend an _____ at your convenience. I look _____ to hearing from you.

Yours _____,

James King.

JAMES KING

6 Some details about writing formal letters in English:

(a) Does James put his name above his address?

(b) Does he write *I'm* or *I am*? *You'll* or *You will*, etc.?

(c) What is his family name?

(d) What is his first name?

(e) Which name does he put first when he signs the letter?

(f) James has never met Mr Rover, so he begins: *Dear Sir*, and finishes: *Yours faithfully*. If he had already met Mr Rover, or if he had corresponded with him, he would begin: *Dear Mr Rover*, and he would finish: *Yours s - n - e - ely*. What is the missing word?

ꕯ

7 You will hear part of James King's interview with Mr Rover, the personnel manager, for the station head waiter's job at Purcell Court. First, make sure you understand the words listed below. Then listen, and note down on a piece of paper the information which Mr Rover gives about:

(a) The hotel

(b) The station head waiter's main duties

(c) The staff for whom he would be responsible

(d) His occasional duties

(e) His hours

(f) Holidays

(g) Fringe benefits

ꕯ

8 Play the tape again. Study and practise James's answers. Follow the procedure for Exercise 7 on page 4.

9 Use the tables below to tell another student or write about your work experience. For example: *I have some experience of working in a bar.*

I have	some a little (quite) a lot of	experience of	working in a bar serving at banquets developing computer programmes etc.

At	... *(former establishment)*	I	learnt basic and other skills served at banquets helped with the training programme developed some new dishes etc.
In	... *(present establishment)*	I	am learning ... am developing ... sometimes/often help ... sometimes/often serve ... etc.

10 You will hear five points that Mr Rover makes at the interview. First, make sure that you understand the beginnings of the sentences below. Then listen and write down the missing words.

1. How would you feel about ...
2. Would you mind ...
3. Would you be prepared to ...
4. I'm afraid you'd have to ...
5. Would you be interested in ...

11 Below are some ways of answering Mr Rover's questions in Exercise 10. Make sure you understand them, and practise saying them. Then play the tape again; this time stop the tape after each question, and give the answer you choose.

I would be very interested in that.
I would enjoy that.
I wouldn't mind that at all.
I wouldn't want to do that, I'm afraid.

12 Use the table on the next page to say or write down what you really think. Compare your statements with other students'.

I	would be very interested in would enjoy wouldn't at all mind	working . . . learning . . . helping . . . developing . . . going . . . etc.
I	wouldn't want to	work . . . go . . . etc.

13   This is a good approach when you apply for a job:

(a) Make a list of what the employer probably wants from the applicants, under these headings:

Education   Qualifications   Experience   Personal qualities

(b) Mention or give evidence of any of these attributes that you really have.
(c) Don't write about anything else.

Here are eight things that someone could write when applying for the job on page 122. Tick (√) the sentences that would be suitable, put a cross (×) by those that would not be suitable. Then discuss your answers with other students.

☐ My present job is uninteresting.
☐ I would like to work in a high-class establishment.
☐ I would like to work in a company that has a lot of hotels abroad.
☐ Your restaurant is close to my home.
☐ Your working hours are convenient.
☐ I am interested in developing my professional skills.
☐ I don't get on with my present Manager.
☐ I am keen to learn about all aspects of restaurant work.

> ## LOCAL AND INTERNATIONAL PLACEMENT SERVICE
> ### Hotel and Catering Division
>
> We are seeking for superior establishments:
>
> **BANQUETING SUPERVISOR,** for conference centre: 50-cover carvery and 150-cover banqueting room.
>
> Enthusiastic young **HEAD WAITER/WAITRESS** with some experience and a knowledge of wines, capable of running a 60-cover à la carte restaurant in the manager's absence.
>
> **CHEF DE RANG** with at least two years' experience in a quality establishment for country house hotel with outstanding reputation for fine cuisine and restaurant service.
>
> **WAITER/WAITRESS** with college training or previous experience for distinguished country house hotel. Good opportunity to become involved in food and drink service and front of house duties.
>
> *Write with two copies of C.V., certificates and recent photograph to:*
>
> LIPS, 6 Cambridge Square, London W1 4GX

Follow-up

14 Work with a partner.

(a) Choose one of the jobs in the advertisement, or use a real advertisement, or write your own advertisement for a job that would be suitable for you.

(b) Together, draw up a list of what the employer probably wants from the applicants, under the headings in Exercise 14.

(c) Check your letters of application (from Exercise 5) for suitable and unsuitable information, as in Exercise 14.

(d) Discuss your letters of application, and improve them if you can.

(e) Write your letter to the employer, like James's in Exercise 5.

(f) Check it for suitable and unsuitable information.

(g) Discuss your letters of application and improve them if you can.

(h) Take turns to be the interviewer and the applicant. Prepare suitable questions. Rôle-play the interviews.

(i) You and your partner can then separate and each work with another student. When you are the interviewer, ask for your new partner's list under (b), and carefully read the advertisement, CV and letter of application. Then interview him or her.

(j) Alternatively, you and your partner can together join another pair. Take turns to be:

A – the interviewer
B – the applicant
C and D – observers, who make notes of the good and bad points in B's performance.

Language reference

Words in a curriculum vitae/CV (Am.E = resumé)
education, qualifications, diplomas, experience, interests, references
Note: For many English-speaking people, *school/high school*, etc. means an establishment which children attend up to the age of 16 or so. An establishment for people of 16 or older is a *college*.

Expressions in letters of application
an application, a (training) course, an interview, a position (*formal*), a job;
to advertise, to apply for a position, to attend a course/interview, to enclose, to include, to offer a position;
Dear Sir(s)/Dear Sir or Madam; Yours faithfully (Am.E = Yours truly)
Dear Mr Rover; Yours sincerely (Am.E = Yours (very) truly)
I look forward to hearing from you. (= I look forward to receiving a letter or phone call.)

Describing the job
main/occasional duties, hours, pay, holidays, fringe benefits, accommodation, a pension, tips, a uniform, a schedule

Describing pay
pay, wages, salary (*for higher levels*)

Describing work experience
I have a little/some/quite a lot of experience of/in serving drinks.

In previous jobs – *past simple*
At the Ritz, I learnt/served/... etc.

In the present job – *present continuous for current activities*
I am learning/developing/... etc.

In the present job – *present simple for regular duties*
I sometimes/often/... serve/work/... etc.

Adverbs of frequency
occasionally, sometimes, often, usually, always

Attitudes towards a possible job
I would be very interested in working in the bar.
I would enjoy serving at banquets.
I wouldn't (at all) mind working on Saturdays.
That would be no problem.
I wouldn't want to work seven days a week, I'm afraid.

Polite questions

Would there be an opportunity to work abroad?

What would my hours be?

Would I be able to/could I work in the bar sometimes?

What would my monthly pay/salary be?

Can staff use the swimming pool?

Transcript of recordings for Units 1–15

Unit 1: Restaurants and their services

Exercise 6

One: A formal, luxury restaurant

WAITER: The Carlton Restaurant. Good morning.
CUSTOMER: Oh, good morning, Can you tell me when you're open?
WAITER: Yes, Sir. We're open for lunch every day except Saturday, and for dinner every day.
CUSTOMER: I see. And what are your hours?
WAITER: Lunch is from twelve-thirty to three, Sir, and dinner from eight until midnight.
CUSTOMER: I see! Thank you.
WAITER: Not at all, Sir.
CUSTOMER: Goodbye!
WAITER: Goodbye, Sir.

Two: The bar in a large international hotel

WAITER: The Capital Bar. Good afternoon!
CUSTOMER: Oh, hello! What are your opening hours?
WAITER: We're open from eleven in the morning till eleven at night, Sir.
CUSTOMER: And I suppose you're open every day.
WAITER: No, Sir. We're closed on Saturdays and Sundays.
CUSTOMER: Oh, I see. Thanks!
WAITER: Not at all, Sir!
CUSTOMER: Goodbye!
WAITER: Goodbye, Sir.

Three: An informal restaurant

WAITER: Hullo! Lorenzo's. Can I help you?
CUSTOMER: Yes, When are you open?
WAITER: We're open seven days a week.

CUSTOMER: What times?
WAITER: Lunch is from twelve to half past three, and dinner from seven till midnight.
CUSTOMER: Thanks!
WAITER: That's all right!
CUSTOMER: Bye!
WAITER: Bye!

Four: The coffee shop in a large international hotel

WAITRESS: The Sugar Cube. Good evening!
CUSTOMER: Oh, hello! I've just flown in. Do I still have time for a snack?
WAITRESS: Yes, Madam. We're open 24 hours a day, seven days a week.
CUSTOMER: Fine! I'll be right down!
WAITRESS: Very good, Madam.

Exercise 13

One

CUSTOMER: What about credit cards? I suppose a Eurocard is OK?
WAITER: Certainly, Madam. We accept Eurocards.

Two

CUSTOMER: Whereabouts are you? I want a bit of peace and quiet — you know, no traffic, no noise. Can I get that in your place?
WAITER: Certainly, Sir. The restaurant is in a very quiet area.

Three

CUSTOMER: Would it be a good idea to reserve a table?
WAITER: Yes, it would. Reservations are advisable.

Four

CUSTOMER: Is there a garden or some place outside to eat?
WAITER: Yes, Sir. You could eat out of doors on our terrace.

Five

CUSTOMER: Is there any music?
WAITER: Yes, there is. There's live music by a guitarist.

Six

CUSTOMER: Any chance of a swim?
WAITER: No, I'm very sorry, Sir. There's no swimming pool here.

Seven

CUSTOMER: Have you got anywhere to park?
WAITER: No, I'm afraid there's no parking here.

Eight

CUSTOMER: Do I need to book?
WAITER: No, Madam. Reservations are not necessary.

Nine

CUSTOMER: Can I use my Diners' Card?
WAITER: No, I'm very sorry. We don't accept Diners' Cards.

Unit 2:   On a restaurant table or tray

Exercise 5, Part A

One

Excuse, me. What's that thing over there?

Two

Say, what are you going to use that pan for?

Three

What've we got these for?

Four

What are these two things on our table, Waiter?

Five

Waiter, what is this, please?

Six

Why is there this flame on the trolley?

Part B

One

CUSTOMER: Excuse me. What's that thing over there?
WAITER: It's an ice bucket, Sir. It's for keeping wine cool.

Two

CUSTOMER: Say, what are you going to use that pan for?
WAITER: It's for flambéeing your crêpe suzette, Sir.

Three

CUSTOMER: What have we got these for?
WAITER: They're for cutting off any grapes you want, Sir.

Four

CUSTOMER: What are these two things on our table, Waiter?
WAITER: They're dish-warmers, Madam. They're for keeping your dishes warm.

Five

CUSTOMER: Waiter, what is this, please?
WAITER: It's a steak knife, Sir. It's for cutting a steak.

Six

CUSTOMER: Why is there this flame on the trolley?
WAITER: It's for cooking your omelette, Madam.

Exercise 9, Part A

One

I say, I'd like to smoke but there's no ash tray on this table.

Two

You know, we could do with some finger bowls here.

Three

Look, can you get me a different fork? This one's bent.

Four

Say! I'm having fish but I haven't got the right knife for it.

Five

Right! You've brought us the wine. How about some glasses?

Six

Room service? The butter knife is missing on our tray.

Seven

Hello! The cup on my breakfast tray is cracked.

Eight

You've sent us up some jam all right, but there's no spoon with it.

Nine

Both the napkins on our tray are stained.

Part B

One

CUSTOMER: I say, I'd like to smoke but there's no ash tray on this table.
WAITER: I'm very sorry, Sir. I'll bring you an ash tray immediately.

Two

CUSTOMER: You know, we could do with some finger bowls here.
WAITRESS: I'm very sorry, Sir. I'll bring you some finger bowls immediately.

Three

CUSTOMER: Look, can you get me a different fork? This one's bent.
WAITER: I'm very sorry, Madam. I'll bring you another fork immediately.

Four

CUSTOMER: Say! I'm having fish but I haven't got the right knife for it.
WAITRESS: I'm very sorry, Sir. I'll bring you a fish knife immediately.

Five

CUSTOMER: Right! You've brought us the wine. How about some glasses?
WAITER: I'm very sorry, Sir. I'll bring you some wine glasses immediately.

Six

CUSTOMER: Room service? The butter knife is missing on our tray.
WAITRESS: I'm very sorry, Sir. We'll send you up a butter knife immediately.

Seven

CUSTOMER: Hullo! The cup on my breakfast tray is cracked.
WAITRESS: I'm very sorry, Madam. We'll send you up another cup immediately.

Eight

CUSTOMER: You've sent us up some jam all right, but there's no spoon with it.
WAITER: I'm very sorry, Sir. We'll send you up a jam spoon immediately.

Nine

CUSTOMER: Both the napkins on our tray are stained.
WAITRESS: I'm very sorry, Sir. We'll send you up some other napkins immediately.

Unit 3: Reservations — 1

Exercise 3, Part A

One

Vaughan.   V - A - U - G - H - A - N

Two

Schnitzer.   S - C - H - N - I - T - Z - E - R

Three

Henriquez.   H - E - N - R - I - Q - U - E - Z

Four

Fakhreldine.   F - A - K - H - R - E - L - D - I - N - E

Five

Neuvillet.   N - E - U - V - I - double L - E - T

Six

Zabokrzecki.   Z - A - B - O - K - R - Z - E - C - K - I

Part B

One

J - A - Y

Two

K - I - N - G

Three

R - I - E - L

Four

H - O - W

Five

F - O - X

Six

M - C - Q - U - double E - N

Exercise 5

One

FIRST CUSTOMER: Oh, hello! I'd like a table for four for lunch today. We'll be arriving at about twelve-thirty. The name is Saarinen; that's S - double A - R - I - N - E - N.

Two

SECOND CUSTOMER: Good afternoon. I want to reserve a table for two for tomorrow evening. That would be for about half-past-eight. My name is De Vienne; D - E -new word- V - I - E - double N - E.

Three

THIRD CUSTOMER: Good evening. I'd like to book a table for dinner on Friday. There'd be eight of us, and we'd get to you at about nine, if that's all right. I'm Dr Al-Dabar. That's A - L -hyphen- D - A - B - A - R.

Exercise 7

WAITER: The Deep Sea Restaurant. Good morning.
MR SAARINEN: Oh, hello! I'd like to book a table.
WAITER: Certainly, sir. For what day would that be?
MR SAARINEN: For today.
WAITER: For today. And for what time would that be?
MR SAARINEN: For about twelve thirty.

WAITER: Twelve thirty. And how many would there be in your party, Sir?
MR SAARINEN: Oh, four.
WAITER: Four. That would be fine. Could I have the name, please?
MR SAARINEN: Saarinen.
WAITER: Could you spell that, please?
MR SAARINEN: S - double A - R - I - N - E - N.
WAITER: Thank you, Sir. So that's a table for four, for today at twelve thirty. We look forward to seeing you.
MR SAARINEN: Thanks! Goodbye!
WAITER: Goodbye, Sir.

Unit 4: Reservations — 2

Exercise 4, Part A

One

FIRST CUSTOMER: I suppose you accept American Express cards? And what about parking?

Two

SECOND CUSTOMER: We're bringing our small daughter. She's two, so we'd need a high chair or something like that. And I wonder if you have a special menu for children.

Three

THIRD CUSTOMER: One member of my party is very lame. He has a wheelchair. Would he be able to get into your restaurant all right?

Four

FOURTH CUSTOMER: We'd all be Muslims in the party, so would there be any difficulties about suitable meat dishes? Do you have Halal meat?

Five

FOURTH CUSTOMER: I'd like a table by the pool, if you've got one. And one of my guests has diabetes. Would he be able to find the right kinds of dishes on your menu?

Part B

One

FIRST CUSTOMER: I suppose you accept American Express cards?
WAITER: Certainly, Madam. That would be no problem.
CUSTOMER: And what about parking?
WAITER: I'm sorry, Madam, there's no parking at the restaurant. But there's a car park in the next street.

Two

SECOND CUSTOMER: We're bringing our small daughter. She's two, so we'd need a high chair or something like that.

WAITER: Certainly, Sir. That would be no problem.

CUSTOMER: And I wonder if you have a special menu for children.

WAITER: No, I'm sorry, Sir, we don't have a children's menu. But your daughter could have small portions of suitable dishes.

Three

THIRD CUSTOMER: One member of my party is very lame. He has a wheelchair. Would he be able to get into your restaurant all right?

WAITER: Certainly, Sir, that would be no problem. We have an elevator.

Four

FOURTH CUSTOMER: We'd all be Muslims in the party, so would there be any difficulties about suitable meat dishes?

WAITER: No, Sir, that would be no problem.

CUSTOMER: Do you have Halal meat?

WAITER: No, I'm sorry, Sir, we have no Halal meat. But we have some excellent fish dishes that would be suitable.

Five

FIFTH CUSTOMER: I'd like a table by the pool, if you've got one.

WAITER: No, I'm sorry, Sir, we have no tables by the pool.

CUSTOMER: And one of my guests has diabetes. Would he be able to find the right kinds of dishes on your menu?

WAITER: Certainly, Sir. That would be no problem.

Exercise 9, Part A

One

FIRST CUSTOMER: I have a reservation for lunch for four today. But we'll be six instead.

Two

SECOND CUSTOMER: We've booked a table for dinner today, but we want to come tomorrow rather than today.

Three

THIRD CUSTOMER: Look, I've got a booking for dinner this evening. It's at nine, but do you think we could bring it forward to eight?

Four

FOURTH CUSTOMER: I'm afraid I've got to cancel my reservation. That's for dinner at eight tomorrow.

Five

FIFTH CUSTOMER: We now think we'd rather be on the terrace than indoors.

Six

SIXTH CUSTOMER: You originally reserved us a table for six. But now there are going to be four extra people. Is that OK?

Part B

One

FIRST CUSTOMER: I have a reservation for lunch for four today. But we'll be six instead.
WAITER: Very good, Sir. Could I have your name please?

Two

SECOND CUSTOMER: We've booked a table for dinner today, but we want to come tomorrow rather than today.
WAITER: I'm very sorry, Madam. We're closed tomorrow.

Three

THIRD CUSTOMER: Look, I've got a booking for dinner this evening. It's at nine, but do you think we could bring it forward to eight?
WAITER: I'm sorry, Sir, we're fully booked at eight. But you could have a table at half past seven.

Four

FOURTH CUSTOMER: I'm afraid I've got to cancel my reservation. That's for dinner at eight tomorrow.
WAITER: Very good, Sir. Could I have your name please?

Unit 5: Directions for finding a restaurant

Exercise 5

WAITRESS: The hotel is not far from the zoo; it's about half a kilometre from the zoo, and it's very near the station. It's opposite the Cedar Hotel, but the entrance is in Duke Street. The coffee shop is on the corner of Cliff Street and Fountain Street. There is a shoe shop next to the coffee shop.

Exercise 7

WAITER: When you leave the theatre, turn left, and go along Hay Street. Go straight on as far as Green Square, then turn left into Park Street. Go past the post office on your left, and go straight on, in the direction of Tor Park. You'll cross Corn Bridge, and just after that, the road forks. Take the right fork; you'll now be in New Road. Then take the third turning on your right; that's Boston Road. You'll see the restaurant on your left. It's just after the hospital and just before the Boston roundabout.

Unit 6: Receiving customers and taking orders

Exercise 4

HEAD WAITER: Good evening, Sir.
GUEST 1: Hi, good evening.

HEAD WAITER: Do you have a reservation?

GUEST 1: Um, yeah, we do.

HEAD WAITER: Could I have your name, please?

GUEST 1: Wanamaker. (*Spells out*) W - A - N - A - M - A - K - E - R.

HEAD WAITER: Mr Wanamaker. Yes, a table for two. Can I take your coats?

GUEST 1: Oh, sure, that'll be fine.

HEAD WAITER: Would you like to come this way? (*Pause*)

WAITER: Good evening, Madam. Good evening, Sir. Would you like an apéritif?

GUEST 2: Mm, I could do with a drink. I think I'll have a gin and tonic.

WAITER: A gin and tonic. With ice, Madam?

GUEST 2: Without.

GUEST 1: And I'll have a dry sherry, please.

WAITER: A dry sherry. Here's the menu. (*Pause. Then sound of glasses being put down.*) Your drinks, Sir.

GUEST 1: Thanks.

WAITER: A roll, Madam?

GUEST 2: Yes, please.

WAITER: Would you like some water?

GUEST 1: No, that's OK.

WAITER: Very good, Sir. (*Pause*) Would you like to order now?

GUEST 1: Hm. I'm not sure.

WAITER: Very good, Sir.

Exercise 8

WAITER: Would you like to order now, Sir?

GUEST 1: Yes, I think we're ready. My friend would like the lamb and I'd like the fillet steak with fried potatoes and a green salad.

WAITER: One lamb and one fillet steak with fried potatoes and a green salad. How would you like your steak done, Sir? Rare, medium, or well done?

GUEST 1: Oh, medium rare, please.

WAITER: Very good, Sir. And would you like anything to start?

GUEST 2: Yes, I'd like a soup.

WAITER: Would you like the vegetable soup or the consommé, Madam?

GUEST 2: Oh, the vegetable, I think.

WAITER: Vetegable soup. And for you, Sir?

GUEST 1: Well, I'm slimming. I'm not too sure.

WAITER: I'd suggest the melon, Sir.

GUEST 1: OK, yes.

WAITER: Have you chosen your wine, Sir?

GUEST 1: Yes, We'll have the St Emilion.

Exercise 11

One

FIRST CUSTOMER: I'd like the poached fresh salmon, but can I have fried potatoes instead of new potatoes?

WAITER: Certainly, Sir.

Two

SECOND CUSTOMER: Grilled Dover sole for me, please. Only, instead of fried potatoes I'd like a green salad.
WAITRESS: Very good, Sir.

Three

THIRD CUSTOMER: This poached breast of chicken sounds nice. But I don't want the rice. Can I have peas instead?
WAITER: I'm very sorry, Madam, that won't be possible. The rice is cooked with the chicken.

Four

FOURTH CUSTOMER: Duck with paté. That sounds interesting. I think I'll have that.
WAITER: I'm very sorry, Sir. There's none left. But I can recommend the roast beef salad.

Five

FIFTH CUSTOMER: Well, I'm going for the cherry and almond tart.
WAITER: I'm very sorry, Madam. We don't have it tonight. But I can recommend the chocolate brandy cake. It's excellent.

Six

SIXTH CUSTOMER: Right. A half-bottle of the St Emilion.
WAITER: I'm very sorry, Sir. We only have whole bottles of the St Emilion. Would you like a carafe of our house wine?

Seven

SEVENTH CUSTOMER: I'd really like the haddock croquettes as a main course, with a mixed salad and peas.
WAITRESS: I don't know if that will be possible, Sir. I'll ask the head waiter.

Unit 7: Explaining dishes: starters and main courses

Exercise 8

List one: chopped onions, mashed potatoes, minced chicken, sliced beetroot, baked carp, poached salmon.
List two: boiled carrots, fried mushrooms, grilled trout, stewed apples, steamed cauliflower.
List three: filleted sole, grated carrots, shredded lettuce.
List four: sauté potatoes, roast lamb.

Exercise 11

One

FIRST CUSTOMER: Can you tell me what this is?
WAITER: Salade breton, Madam? It's a salad. It consists of chopped carrots, French beans, potatoes, and turnips, with hard-boiled eggs, mayonnaise and French dressing.
FIRST CUSTOMER: I see. And are the vegetables raw?
WAITER: No, Madam, they're cooked.

Two

SECOND CUSTOMER: What's this?

WAITRESS: Vichyssoise, Sir? It's a creamy soup made of leeks, onions and potatoes, with cream.

SECOND CUSTOMER: Is it hot?

WAITRESS: No, Sir, it's cold.

Three

THIRD CUSTOMER: Do you think you could explain this dish to me?

WAITER: Moussaka? Certainly. It's a sort of pie; it's made of minced lamb, sliced aubergines, onions and tomatoes, with eggs and cream.

THIRD CUSTOMER: Is there any garlic in it?

WAITER: No, there isn't.

Unit 8: During the meal

Exercise 5

Number 1

WAITER: Your soup, Madam.

CUSTOMER: Oh, yes. Not too much, please.

WAITER: Some croutons?

WAITER: Hm – I'm slimming. I'd better not.

Number 2

WAITER: Your soup, Sir.

CUSTOMER: Splendid! Plenty, please.

WAITER: Some croutons?

CUSTOMER: Mm! I think I'll try some of those.

Number 3

WAITER: Your soup, Sir.

CUSTOMER: Fine! Thanks!

WAITER: Some croutons?

CUSTOMER: Just a couple, thanks.

Number 4

WAITER: Your beef, Madam.

CUSTOMER: Oh, I'd like a good-sized helping of that.

WAITER: Some potatoes?

CUSTOMER: Mm, lots, please.

Number 5

WAITER: Your beef, Sir.

CUSTOMER: A tiny slice, thanks.

WAITER: Some potatoes?

CUSTOMER: Oh, erm, I don't want many.

Number 6

WAITER: Your beef, Sir.
CUSTOMER: Oh, go easy with it, please.
WAITER: Some potatoes?
CUSTOMER: Potatoes? I won't have any, thanks.

Exercise 6

Number 1

CUSTOMER: Waiter!
WAITER: Yes, Madam?
CUSTOMER: Do you think we could have some rolls?
WAITER: Certainly, Madam.
CUSTOMER: We don't need any butter, but some grated cheese would be nice.
WAITER: Certainly, Madam. I'll get you some.

Number 2

CUSTOMER: Excuse me! Waitress!
WAITRESS: Yes, Sir?
CUSTOMER: We'd like some mineral water, with plenty of ice in it. And my friend here would like a cup of black coffee while we're waiting for the next course.
WAITRESS: Certainly, Sir. I'll get you some.

Number 3

CUSTOMER: Excuse me!
WAITER: Yes, Sir?
CUSTOMER: Have you got a light?
WAITER: I'll bring you some matches straightaway, Sir.
CUSTOMER: Thanks! And there's no salt on this table.
WAITER: I'm very sorry, Sir. I'll get some straightaway.

Number 4

CUSTOMER: I say!
WAITER: Yes, Sir?
CUSTOMER: All these rolls are white. Do you have any brown ones instead?
WAITER: No, I'm very sorry, Sir, we haven't.
CUSTOMER: Oh, well, never mind. And we'd like some mint jelly to go with our lamb.
WAITER: I'm very sorry, Sir, we don't have that. Perhaps you'd like some parsley butter instead?

Unit 9: Later stages of the meal

Exercise 7

One: sliced oranges
Two: baked apples

Three: stewed plums
Four: tinned peaches
Five: chopped walnuts
Six: ground almonds
Seven: grated nutmeg
Eight: shredded coconut
Nine: mixed dried fruit
Ten: whipped cream
Eleven: beaten egg yolks
Twelve: beaten egg whites
Thirteen: pears poached in red wine
Fourteen: sliced apples dipped in batter
Fifteen: pieces of fresh fruit

Exercise 8

Apple Charlotte. It's a cold pudding. It consists of cooked, sliced apples, breadcrumbs and slices of bread. It's flavoured with cinnamon and it's served with apricot sauce.

Apricot Amber. It's a hot fruit pie. It consists of apricots and beaten egg yolks in pastry, with beaten egg whites on top.

Malakoff Pudding. It's a cold sweet. It consists of a mixture of fruit, ground almonds, egg yolks and cream, with lady finger biscuits. It's flavoured with rum.

Exercise 16

Order number one

We'd like some coffee right now, while we're waiting for our meal. That'll be one white and two black. Oh, and can we have milk for the white instead of cream?

Order number two

We'd like our coffee with our dessert, please. That's two decaffeinated with cream, one espresso and a capuccino. OK? And do you have any saccharine?

Order number three

I think I'll try this Turkish coffee. Sounds kind of exciting. And my friend here says he'll go for the Irish. But we'll have our sweets first, please.

Exercise 17

WAITER: Will that be sufficient, Madam?
WOMAN CUSTOMER: Oh, yes, thank you, I've finished. That was delicious.
WAITER: Thank you, Madam. I'm glad you enjoyed it. Would you like a dessert now, or some cheese?
WOMAN CUSTOMER: Yes, I think I'll have the fruit salad.
MAN CUSTOMER: And I'll have cheese and crackers.
(Later)
WAITER: Would you like some coffee now?

MAN CUSTOMER: Yes, please. Both black.
WAITER: Would you like some liqueurs?
MAN CUSTOMER: Yes, my friend will have a Tia Maria and I'll have a Cointreau.

Unit 10: Drinks

Exercise 5

One

I'll have a large gin and tonic, please. No ice, and just a splash of tonic.

Two

I could do with a good, stiff brandy.

Three

Can you get me a vodka and orange? Give me plenty of ice, would you?

Four

Whisky and soda, please. With ice. And go easy on the soda. (*Sound of soda siphon.*) Hey, don't drown it!

Five

I'd like a double brandy and soda. Make it a long drink, will you. (*Sound of soda siphon.*) Yeah, better fill it up.

Exercise 9

One

WAITER: Good afternoon, Sir. What would you like?
CUSTOMER: We'll have one gin and tonic, two Scotch on the rocks, and a tonic with ice.
WAITER: Certainly, Sir. (*Pause.*) Here you are, Sir.
CUSTOMER: Thank you. How much is that?
WAITER: That'll be eight pounds fifty, Sir.

Two

WAITER: Good evening, Madam. What can I get you?
CUSTOMER: We'd like two rum and Cokes, a gin, a bitter lemon, a Seven-up and a vodka with orange.
WAITER: Thank you, Madam.

Three

WAITER: Good evening, Sir. Would you like anything to drink?
CUSTOMER: Yes, can you bring us three cokes, a Perrier, a small sherry, and a brandy and soda.
WAITER: Very good, Sir. Will that be a dry or sweet sherry?
CUSTOMER: Medium dry, please.

Unit 11: Talking about money

Exercise 3

(a) twelve; fourteen; forty; fifty-two; a hundred and thirty-seven; two hundred and eighty-six; one thousand, four hundred and seventy-three.
(b) five plus thirteen; twenty-two minus four; eight times eleven, or eight multiplied by eleven; forty-five divided by nine.
(c) ten point five; fifteen per cent; a hundred and ninety-three less ten per cent; sixteen dollars fifty.
(d) twenty less eight per cent; fifteen percent of two thousand and forty-five; six dollars forty-five multiplied by three; three hundred and eighty-five plus twenty-seven.

Exercise 6

One

FIRST CUSTOMER: I don't have any francs. Is it OK if I pay in US dollars?
WAITER: Certainly, Sir.

Two

SECOND CUSTOMER: I'd like to use my Visa card, if that's OK.
WAITER: Certainly, Madam. That'll be fine.

Three

THIRD CUSTOMER: I've got a whole lot of your currency I want to use up, so I think I'll pay with that.
WAITER: Certainly, Sir.

Four

FOURTH CUSTOMER: Are these American Express traveller's cheques OK with you?
WAITER: What currency are they, Madam?
FOURTH CUSTOMER: Pounds sterling.
WAITER: I'm very sorry, Madam. We only accept traveller's cheques in dollars.
FOURTH CUSTOMER: Oh, well, then I'd better use the cash I've got left.

Five

FIFTH CUSTOMER: Hm. Can I pay by cheque? Here's my banker's card.
WAITER: I'm very sorry, Sir. We don't accept banker's cards. Do you have an international credit card?

Six

SIXTH CUSTOMER: Can I use these German marks? You see, I've got very few pesetas left.
WAITER: I'm not sure, Sir. I'll just ask the cashier.

Exercise 11

CUSTOMER: Could I have my bill, please?
WAITER: Certainly, Sir. One moment, please. (*Pause.*) Here's your bill, Sir.

CUSTOMER: Thank you. What's this item here? Number 1.
WAITER: That's the cover charge, Sir.
CUSTOMER: I see. And what's this? Item 6.
WAITER: That's the vegetables with your chicken, Sir.
CUSTOMER: Oh, the vegetables weren't included?
WAITER: No, Sir. They were extra.
CUSTOMER: OK. Now — I don't understand this: you seem to have charged me twice for the dessert. Look at items 8 and 10.
WAITER: I'll just go and check it for you, Sir. (*Pause.*) Yes, Sir, you're right. The cashier made a mistake. I think you'll find it's correct now.
CUSTOMER: Thank you.
WAITER: We're very sorry about this.
CUSTOMER: Oh, that's all right. Now: can I pay by traveller's cheques?
WAITER: Certainly, Sir. We'll give you the change in local currency, if that's all right.
CUSTOMER: Oh, keep the change.
WAITER: Thank you very much indeed, Sir.
CUSTOMER: And I'd like a receipt.
WAITER: Certainly, Sir.

Unit 12: Complaints and other problems

Exercise 5

One

CUSTOMER: Say, waiter! It's terribly cold by this window. Just feel the draught! Can you find us another table?
WAITER: Yes, I'm sorry, Sir. I'll ask the Head Waiter about another table. I'm sure we can find you something more suitable.

Two

HEAD WAITER: Is there a problem, Madam?
CUSTOMER: Yes, there certainly is. We arrived twenty minutes ago and we still haven't even seen the menu. The service here is appalling.
HEAD WAITER: I'm extremely sorry, Madam. There must be some mistake. I'll send you a waiter immediately, and we'll make sure you enjoy your meal.

Three

CUSTOMER: Say, waiter! I'm not happy with this steak.
WAITER: I'm very sorry, Sir. What's the problem?
CUSTOMER: I asked for it well done, and it's completely rare.
WAITER: I'm so sorry, Sir. There must be some mistake. I'll change it for you immediately.

Four

CUSTOMER: Excuse me. I really can't eat this fish. It's off.
WAITER: I'm very sorry, Madam. I'll take it away. Would you like to order something else?

Five

CUSTOMER: Look! You've spilt soup all over my dress!
WAITER: I'm extremely sorry, Madam. I'll bring some water and a napkin . . .
CUSTOMER: No! I want to speak to the Manager!
WAITER: Very good, Madam.
MANAGER: I'm extremely sorry about this, Madam. We'll be happy to pay your cleaning bill, of course.
CUSTOMER: Oh, you will? In that case . . .

Six

CUSTOMER: What do you mean, you're full and there's no table in my name? I rang this afternoon and made a reservation.
HEAD WAITER: I'm very sorry, Sir. There must be some mistake. But we have a pleasant table in the Blue Room.
CUSTOMER: But I don't want to be in the Blue Room. I want a table here.
HEAD WAITER: I'm afraid that won't be possible, Sir.
CUSTOMER: Well, I find this really irritating.
HEAD WAITER: I understand how you feel, Sir. But we'll try to make sure you enjoy your meal.

Unit 13: Banqueting arrangements

Exercise 5

BANQUETING MANAGER: Good afternoon. Tessa Williams, Forest Hotel Banqueting Manager. Can I help you?
CUSTOMER: Yes, this is James Richardson, International Consultants Ltd. I'm phoning to enquire if you could cater for a reception we're planning.
BANQUETING MANAGER: I see. For what day would that be, Mr Richardson?
CUSTOMER: February 1st.
BANQUETING MANAGER: February 1st. And for what time of the day?
CUSTOMER: The evening.
BANQUETING MANAGER: What sort of function would it be, Mr Richardson?
CUSTOMER: It'll be a dinner party for our sales personnel from abroad.
BANQUETING MANAGER: I see. And how many people would there be?
CUSTOMER: There'll be about twenty of us.
BANQUETING MANAGER: Yes, that would be possible.
CUSTOMER: I think your Fountain Room would be suitable.
BANQUETING MANAGER: Yes, that's free then. It's a very pleasant room. How much per head would you like to spend, Mr Richardson?
CUSTOMER: Around £20.
BANQUETING MANAGER: Would that include drinks, or would they be extra?
CUSTOMER: Oh, they'd be extra.
BANQUETING MANAGER: Yes, well, that would be fine. I'll confirm those details in writing to you. Do you have our banqueting information pack, Mr Richardson?
CUSTOMER: No, I don't.

BANQUETING MANAGER: Then I'll send it to you with my letter of confirmation. You'll find a set of menus and a wine list in it. We can discuss the menu and wines and any further details after you've seen it. Could I have your address and telephone number, please?
CUSTOMER: Yes, of course. It's ...

Exercise 9

CUSTOMER 1: What size is your Statesman Two room?
BANQUETING MANAGER: Our Statesman Two room? It's about $5\frac{1}{2}$ metres square.
CUSTOMER 2: What do you charge for microphones?
BANQUETING MANAGER: There would be no charge for microphones.
CUSTOMER 3: We'd like a video recorder. How much would that be?
BANQUETING MANAGER: The charge would be £10 per day.

Now answer the next five questions yourself. You will hear a tone (TONE) after each question. Stop the tape and speak. Then start the tape again.

One

CUSTOMER 4: We'll be needing an overhead projector. What do you charge for that? (TONE)

Two

CUSTOMER 5: I think a flip chart would be useful. How much would that be? (TONE)

Three

CUSTOMER 6: Now then. How big is your Statesman Three room? (TONE)

Four

CUSTOMER 7: We'd like a blackboard if it's not too expensive. What would you charge for that? (TONE)

Five

CUSTOMER 8: Can you tell me roughly how large your Statesman One room is? (TONE)

Unit 14: Breakfast

Exercise 3

Customer 1

CUSTOMER 1: I'd like the Continental breakfast, please.
WAITRESS: Yes, certainly, Madam.
CUSTOMER 1: With orange juice.
WAITRESS: With orange juice. And what beverage would you like, Madam?
CUSTOMER 1: Oh, I guess I'll have the decaffeinated coffee.

Customer 2

WAITRESS: Which breakfast would you like, Sir?
CUSTOMER 2: Oh, I'll have the Health breakfast, I think.

WAITRESS: Right, Sir. How would you like your egg done?
CUSTOMER 2: Mm, boiled.
WAITRESS: How many minutes, Sir?
CUSTOMER 2: Three. No, make it four.
WAITRESS: Very good, Sir.

Customer 3

CUSTOMER 3: This May Fair breakfast looks pretty terrific. I think I'll go for that.
WAITRESS: Fine, Sir. What juice would you like? Orange or grapefruit?
CUSTOMER 3: Um, grapefruit. And I'll have coffee, please.

Exercise 6

WAITRESS: Good morning, Sir. Are you ready to order?
CUSTOMER: Yes, thanks. I'll have the English breakfast.
WAITRESS: Very good, Sir.
CUSTOMER: I'll have grapefruit juice, to begin with.
WAITRESS: Grapefruit juice. And then would you like cereal, fruit or yoghurt?
CUSTOMER: Cereal, please. What cereals do you have?
WAITRESS: We have Rice Krispies, All Bran, Weetabix, cornflakes and porridge.
CUSTOMER: Weetabix, please. And I'll have my eggs scrambled.
WAITRESS: Scrambled. What would you like your eggs served with, Sir? Bacon or ham?
CUSTOMER: Bacon, please. And I won't have the sausage but I'd like the tomato.
WAITRESS: Very good, Sir. And what would you like to drink?
CUSTOMER: Tea, please.

Exercise 8

CUSTOMER: Good morning!
(PAUSE)
CUSTOMER: Yes, I am. I'll have orange juice please.
(PAUSE)
CUSTOMER: I don't think I want any cereal. I'll have one of your fruit dishes. Let me see. What have you got?
(PAUSE)
CUSTOMER: Right. I'll have the fruit salad. Then I'll have boiled eggs.
(PAUSE)
CUSTOMER: Three minutes, please.
(PAUSE)
CUSTOMER: Oh, nothing, thanks. I'll have them on their own. And what drinks do you have?
(PAUSE)
CUSTOMER: OK. I'll have decaffeinated coffee. Right! Thanks very much.

Unit 15: Applying for jobs

Exercise 7

MR ROVER: Come in, please. Ah, James King?
JAMES: Yes, that's right, Sir.
MR ROVER: Hello!
JAMES: Good afternoon, Sir.
MR ROVER: Do sit down.
JAMES: Thank you.
MR ROVER: Right. Well, now, I wonder – what do you know about Purcell Court?
JAMES: I know that it's part of the Inter-Metropolitan chain, that it has a high-class clientèle, and that most of the work is for conferences.
MR ROVER: Yes, that's right. We have 42 bedrooms, and six de luxe suites. The restaurant seats 60 covers. There are three bars and a lounge, and there's also a swimming pool, a squash court, and a golf course. Then, um, let's see … your duties. Your main duties would be the total service for six tables, that would be twenty covers. And you'd be responsible for a staff of three: a chef de rang and two commis waiters. How would you feel about that?
JAMES: I think I could manage that quite well, Sir. What would the occasional duties be?
MR ROVER: Well, you'd have to cover for the barman sometimes. How would you feel about that?
JAMES: I would enjoy that, Sir. I have some experience of working in a hotel bar, and I took a course in bar work last year.
MR ROVER: Yes, so I see from your CV. Then there would be other occasional duties: you'd have late duty every four days, and you might have to cover for the Breakfast Head Waiter sometimes. Would that be OK?
JAMES: Yes, I wouldn't mind that at all, Sir.
MR ROVER: Right, then, the hours. You'd work 40 hours, five days a week, with your days off on rota. On three days a week you'd do breakfast and lunch, one day a week lunch and dinner, and one day a week dinner only. Right?
JAMES: Yes, Sir.
MR ROVER: Then holidays. There'd be four weeks a year.
JAMES: I see.
MR ROVER: And there are some fringe benefits, of course. For example, staff can use the swimming pool and squash courts at certain times. Also they can get a company card which gives them a discount in some shops. And of course, the staff meals are excellent. Now then, do you have any questions?
JAMES: Yes, Sir. Would there be an opportunity to work abroad with the chain?
MR ROVER: You'd like to work abroad, would you?
JAMES: Yes, I'd be very interested in that.
MR ROVER: Well, yes, certainly. Mm, I see you're studying French, so that would be a help. Yes, the chain has three hotels in France, one in French Switzerland, … (FADE)

Exercise 10

1. How would you feel about working in the kitchen sometimes?
2. Would you mind covering for other people when they're sick?
3. Would you be prepared to work late two days a week?
4. I'm afraid you'd have to work three week-ends out of four.
5. Would you be interested in going on any training courses?

APPENDIX 2

Student B's part in pair work exercises

Unit 1, Exercise 17

Student B

(a) You are a tourist phoning The Pacific Restaurant, a formal, four-star restaurant, for information. You ask these questions:

Do you have a set menu?
How much is a typical three-course à la carte lunch?
Do you have anywhere to park?
Is there a band or something like that?
Can we eat outside?
Do I need to make a reservation?
When are you open for lunch?

(b) You work in this informal restaurant.

The Merida ** Set £10 L £15 D   Res CrC: A.Ex. Eur Vi DC

Student A, a tourist, rings you for information.
Describe the restaurant and answer his/her questions.
Use language from Exercises 2, 6, 8, 9 and 12.
Begin: 'The Merida. Can I help you?'

Unit 3, Exercise 11

Student B

(a) You work at the Deep Sea Restaurant. Student A, a customer, rings to make a reservation. Politely ask the following questions and make the requests. Note down the information.
   What day?
   What time?
   How many people?
   Table near the band?
   Name?
   How do you spell that?
   Repeat that.

(b) You are Dr Al-Dabar (in Exercise 5), and you are on the telephone to the Deep Sea Restaurant, where Student A is a waiter/waitress. Answer his/her questions.

(c) Continue as in (a) and (b), but in (b) pretend to be different customers, and be ready to answer B's questions.

Unit 7, Exercise 17

Student B

(a) You are a customer. A is a waiter/waitress. Use the customer's words in Exercise 16 to ask B about Ratatouille.

(b) You are a waiter/waitress. A, a customer, will ask you questions about Wiener Schnitzel. Use the waiter's words in Exercise 16 to help you to explain it.

   Wiener Schnitzel: fried veal
   Main ingredient: veal
   Additional ingredients: flour, egg yolks, breadcrumbs
   Preparation: slice veal very thinly
   Method of cooking: dip veal in flour, egg yolks and breadcrumbs; then fry in butter.
   Accompaniments: serve with sauté potatoes and a green salad

Unit 13, Exercise 10

Student B

(a) You are John/Jane Long, the Sales Manager of International Hire-a-Car Inc., and you are discussing details about a dinner dance for company executives with A, a banqueting manager. Answer A's questions.

   This is what you want:

   1. Table service
   2. Small individual tables for 4
   3. No place cards

4. A small band and dancing
5. Red, white and blue flowers
6. Menu cards decorated with an antique car
7. A photographer
8. The bill should be sent to you

(b) You are a banqueting manager, and student A is John/Janet King, Marketing Manager of Far Eastern Travel Ltd. Ask these questions, and note A's answers. You will use your notes in Exercise 11.

1. What sort of service would you like?
2. What about music?
3. What sort of table decorations would you like?
4. What sort of design would you like for the menus?
5. Would you like a photographer?
6. Do you have any special wishes as regards food?
7. How will you be paying?

List of ingredients and processes

The following abbreviations are used:
u = uncountable; c = countable; pl = plural; Am.E = American English

English	French	Spanish
Meat	*Viandes*	*Carnes*
bacon (*u*)	lard	tocino
beef (*u*)	boeuf	res
ham (*u*)	jambon	jamón
lamb (*u*)	agneau	cordero
mutton (*u*)	mouton	carnero
pork (*u*)	porc	cerdo
veal (*u*)	veau	ternera
Offal	*Abats*	*Menudos*
brains (*c, pl*)	cervelle	sesos
heart (*u/c*)	coeur	corazón
kidney (*u/c*)	rognon	riñon
liver (*u/c*)	foie	hígado
oxtail (*u*)	queue de boeuf	rabo de vaca
sweetbread (*u*)	ris	mollejas
tongue (*u/c*)	langue	lengua

Italian	German	Greek
Carni	*Fleisch*	Κρέατα
pancetta/guanciale	Speck	μπέκον (χοιρομέρι, καπνιστό, χοιρινό)
manzo	Rindfleisch	βωδινό
prosciutto	Schinken	ζαμπόν
agnello	Lammfleisch	αρνάκι
montone	Hammelfleisch	αρνί
maiale	Schweinefleisch	χοιρινό
vitello	Kalbfleisch	μοσχαράκι
Frattaglie	*Innereien*	Εντόσθια
cervello	Hirn	μυαλά
cuore	Herz	καρδιά
rognone	Niere	νεφρά
fegato	Leber	συκώτι
coda di bue	Ochsenschwanz	ουρά βωδινή
animelle	Bries	αμελέτητα
lingua	Zunge	γλώσσα

English	**French**	**Spanish**
Poultry	*Volaille*	*Aves*
chicken (*u/c*)	poulet	pollo
duck (*u/c*)	canard	pato
duckling (*u/c*)	caneton	pato joven
goose (*u/c*)	oie	ganso
pigeon (*u/c*)	pigeon	pichón
turkey (*u/c*)	dinde	pavo
Game	*Gibier*	*Caza*
hare (*u/c*)	lièvre	liebre
partridge (*u/c*)	perdreau	perdiz
pheasant (*u/c*)	faisan	faisán
quail (*u/c*)	caille	cordoniz
rabbit (*u/c*)	lapin	conejo
venison (*u*)	chevreuil	ciervo, venado
Fish	*Poisson*	*Pescados*
anchovy (*u/c*) (-ies)	anchois	boquerones
carp (*u/c*)	carpe	carpa
caviar (*u*)	caviar	caviar
cod (*u*)	cabillaud	bacalao fresco
eel (*u/c*)	anguille	anguila
haddock (*fresh*) (*u*)	aiglefin	abadejo
halibut (*u*)	flétan	halibut (*hipogloso*)
herring (*u/c*)	hareng	arenque
plaice (*u/c*)	plie	platija
roe (*u/c*)	laitance, oeufs	lecha, lechaza
sardine (*c*)	sardine	sardina
salmon (*u/c*)	saumon	salmón
trout (*u/c*)	truite	trucha
turbot (*u*)	turbot	rodaballo
tuna (*u*) (Am.E = tunny fish)	thon	atún
whitebait (*u*)	blanchaille	chanquetes

Italian	German	Greek
Pollame	*Gefrügel*	Πουλερικά
pollo	Huhn	κοτόπουλο
anitra	Ente	πάπια
anitra novella	Junge Ente	παπάκι
oca	Gans	χήνα
piccione	Taube	πιτσούνι
Tacchino	Truthahn, Puter	γαλοπούλα
Cacciagione	*Wildbret*	Κυνήγι
lepre	Hase	λαγός
pernice	Rebhuhn	πέρδικα
fagiano	Fasan	φασιανός
quaglia	Wachteln	ορτύκι
coniglio	Kaninchen	κουνέλι
cervo	Hirsch	ζαρκάδι
Pesci	*Fisch*	Ψάρια
acciuga	Sardellen	αντσούγιες
carpa	Karpfen	κυπρίνος (σαζάνι)
caviale	Kaviar	χαβιάρι
baccalá (merluzzo)	Kabeljau	μπακαλιάρος
anguilla	Aal	χέλι
dentice/eglefino	Schellfisch	γάδος
halibut	Heilbutt	ιππόγλωσσος
aringa	Hering	ρέγγα
sogliola/platessa	Scholle	πησσί
uova di pesce	Rogen	αυγοτάραχο
sardine	Sardinen	σαρδέλα
salmone	Lachs	σολωμός
trota	Forelle	πέστροφα
rombo	Steinbutt	καλκάμι, συάκι
tonno	Thunfisch	τόννος
bianchetti	Weißfische	μαρίδα

English	**French**	**Spanish**
Shellfish, etc.	*Crustacés, etc.*	*Crustáceos, etc.*
clams (*c, pl*)	palourdes	almejas
crab (*u/c*)	crabe	cangrejo de mar
crawfish (*u/c*)	langouste	langosta
crayfish (*u/c*)	écrevisse	cangrejo
lobster (*u/c*)	homard	bogavante
mussels (*c, pl*)	moules	mejillones
octopus (*u*)	poulpe	pulpo
oysters (*c, pl*)	huîtres	ostras
prawns (*c, pl*)	crevettes roses	gambas
scallop (*c*)	coquille St Jacques	concha de peregrino
scampi (*c, pl*)	langoustines	cigalas
shrimps (*c, pl*)	crevettes grises	camarones
Vegetables	*Légumes*	*Verduras*
artichoke (*c*)	artichaut	alcachofa
asparagus (*u*)	asperges	esparragos
aubergine (*u/c*) (Am.E = eggplant)	aubergine	berenjena
avocado (*u/c*)	avocat	aguacate
beans (*broad*) (*c, pl*)	fèves	habas
beans (*french*) (*c, pl*)	haricots verts	judías verdes
beetroot (*u/c*)	betterave	remolacha
broccoli (*u*)	brocolis	brécoles
Brussels sprouts (*c, pl*)	choux de Bruxelles	coles de Bruselas
cabbage (*u*)	chou	col
carrots (*c*)	carottes	zanahorias
cauliflower (*u*)	chou-fleur	coliflor
celery (*u*)	céleri	apio
corn on the cob (*u*)	maïs en épi	mazorca de maíz
courgettes (*c*)	courgettes	calabacines

Italian	German	Greek
Crostacei	*Schaltiere*	Οστρακοειδή κ.λ.π.
vongole	Venusmuscheln	αχηβάδες
granchi	Strandkrabben	καβούρι
gamberoni	Languste	
gamberi	Krebse	καραβίδα
aragosta/leone di mare	Hummer	αστακός
cozze	Miesmuscheln	μύδια
polpo	Krake	χταπόδι
ostriche	Austern	στρείδια
gamberetti	Steingarnelen	γαρίδες
conchiglie del pellegrino	Jakobsmuscheln	χτένια
scampi	Scampi	γαρίδες τηγανητές
gamberetti grigi	Garnelen	γαριδάκια
Verdure	*Gemüse*	Λαχανικά
carciofo	Artischocke	αγκινάρα
asparagi	Spargel	σπαράγκια
melanzane	Aubergine	μελιτζάνες
avocado	Avocado	αβοκάντο
fave	Saubohnen	κουκιά
fagiolini	Grüne Bohnen	φασολάκια
carota rossa/ barbabietola	Rote Rübe	παντζάρια
broccoli	Brokkoli	μπρόκολα
broccoletti di Bruxelles	Rosenkohl	λαχανάκια
cavolo	Kohl	λάχανο
carote	Karotten	καρρότα
cavolfiore	Blumenkohl	κουνουπίδι
sedano	Sellerie	σέλινο
pannocchia di granturco	Maiskolben	γλυκό καλαμπόκι
zucchine	Zucchini	κολοκυθάκια

English	French	Spanish

Vegetables (cont.)

English	French	Spanish
cucumber (*u*)	concombre	pepino
leeks (*u*)	poireaux	puerros
lettuce (*u*)	laitue	lechuga
mushrooms (*c*)	champignons	champiñones
olives (*c*)	olives	aceitunas
onion (*u/c*)	oignon	cebolla
peas (*c, pl*)	petits pois	guisantes
potatoes (*u/c*) (-es)	pommes de terre	patatas
baked potatoes (*c*)	pommes de terre au four	patatas asadas al horno
potato chips (*c, pl*)	pommes frites	patatas fritas
mashed potatoes (*u/c, pl*)	purée de pommes de terre	puré de patatas
radish (*c*) (-es)	radis	rabanitos
spinach (*u*)	épinards	espinacas
tomato (*u/c*) (-es)	tomate	tomate
turnip (*u/c*)	navet	nabo
watercress (*u*)	cresson	berros

Fruits | *Fruits .* | *Frutas*

English	French	Spanish
apple (*u/c*)	pomme	manzana
apricot (*c*)	abricot	albaricoque
banana (*u/c*)	banane	plátano
blackberry (*c*) (-es)	mûre	zarzamora
black currant (*c, pl*)	cassis	grosella negra
red currant (*c, pl*)	groseille rouge	grosella roja
cherry (*c*) (-ies)	cerise	cereza
date (*c*)	datte	datil
fig (*c*)	figue	higo
grapefruit (*u/c*)	pamplemousse	toronja
grape (*c*)	raisin	uva
lemon (*u/c*)	citron	limón
melon (*u/c*)	melon	melón

Italian	German	Greek
cetriolo	Gurke	αγγούρι
porri	Porree	πράσα
lattuga	Kopfsalat	μαρούλι
funghi	Pilze	μανιτάρια
olive	Oliven	εληές
cipolla	Zwiebel	κρεμύδια
piselli	Erbsen	μπιζέλια
patate	Kartoffeln	πατάτες
patate intere al forno	Kartoffeln in der Schale gebraten	πατάτες ψητές
patatine fritte	Pommes frites	πατάτες τηγανητές
puré di patate	Kartoffelpüree	πατάτες πουρέ
ravanelli	Radieschen	ρεπανάκια
spinaci	Spinat	σπανάκι
pomodoro	Tomate	ντομάτες
rapa	Rübe	ράπα (γογγύλι)
crescione	Kreße	αντράκλα (νεροκάρδαμο)

Frutta	*Obst*	Φρούτα
mela	Apfel	μήλα
albicocca	Aprikose	βερύκοκα
banana	Banane	μπανάνες
mora	Brombeere	βατόμουρα
mirtillo	schwarze Johannisbeere	φραγκοστάφυλα
mirtillo rosso	rote Johannisbeere	κόκκινη σταφίδα
ciliegia	Kirsche	κεράσια
dattero	Dattel	χουρμάδες
fico	Feige	σύκα
pompelmo	Grapefruit	αγριόφραππα
uva	Trauben	σταφύλια
limone	Zitrone	λεμόνι
melone	Melone	πεπόνι

English	**French**	**Spanish**

Fruits (cont.)

English	French	Spanish
orange (*u/c*)	orange	naranja
peach (*c*) (-es)	pêche	melocotón
pear (*c*)	poire	pera
pineapple (*u/c*)	ananas	ananás, piña
plum (*c*)	prune	ciruela
raspberry (*c*) (-ies)	framboise	frambuesa
strawberry (*c*) (-ies)	fraise	fresa
water melon (*u/c*)	pastèque	sandía

Nuts — *Noix* — *Nueces*

English	French	Spanish
almond (*c*)	amande	almendra
Brazil nut (*c*)	noix de Brésil	castaña de Pará
chestnut (*c*)	marron	castaña
coconut (*u/c*)	noix de coco	coco
hazelnut (*c*)	noisette	avellana
pecan (*c*)	pacane	pacana
pistachio (*c*)	pistache	pistacho
peanut (*c*)	cacahuète	cacahuete
walnut (*c*)	noix	nuez

Eggs — *Oeufs* — *Huevos*

English	French	Spanish
boiled eggs (*c*)	oeufs à la coque	huevos pasados por agua
soft boiled eggs (*c*)	oeufs mollets	huevos blandos
hard boiled eggs (*c*)	oeufs durs	huevos duros
fried eggs (*c*) (Am.E = eggs sunny side up)	oeufs sur le plat	huevos estrellados
poached eggs (*c*)	oeufs pochés	huevos escafaldos
scrambled eggs (*c*)	oeufs brouillés	huevos revueltos
egg white/white of egg (*u*)	blanc d'oeuf	clara de huevo
egg yolk/yolk of egg (*u*)	jaune d'oeuf	yema de huevo

Italian	German	Greek
arancia	Orange	πορτοκάλια
pesca	Pfirsich	ροδάκινα
pera	Birne	αχλάδια
ananas	Ananas	ανανάς
prugna/susina	Pflaume	δαμάσκηνα
lampone	Himbeere	σμέουρα
fragola	Erdbeere	φράουλες
anguria/cocomero	Wassermelone	καρπούζι
Noci	*Nüße*	*Ξηροί καρποί*
mandorla	Mandel	αμύγδαλα
noce brasiliana	Brasilnuß	Βραζιλιανά καρύδια
castagna/marrone	Marone	κάστανα
noce di cocco	Kokosnuß	Ινδική καρύδα
nocciola	Haselnuß	φουντούκια
noce americana	Pekannuß	πεκάν
pistacchio	Pistazie	φυστίκι Αιγίνης
nocciolina americana	Erdnuß	Αράπικο φυστίκι
noce	Walnuß	καρύδια
Uova	*Eierspeisen*	*Αυγά*
uova al guscio/alla coque	weiche Eier (3 mn)	αυγό βραστό
uova bazzote	weiche Eier (6 mn)	αυγό μελάτο
uova sode	hart gekochte Eier	αυγό βραστό σκληρό
uova al piatto/uova fritte	Spiegeleier	αυγό τηγανητό
uova affogate/in camicia	pochierte Eier	αυγό ποσέ
uova strapazzate	Rühreier	αυγό στραπατσάδα
chiara d'uovo/albume	Eiweiß	ασπράδι αυγού
rosso d'uovo/tuorlo	Eigelb	κροκάδι αυγου

English	French	Spanish
Dairy products	*Produits laitiers*	*Productos lácteos*
cream (*u*)	crème	nata, crema
cheese (*u*)	fromage	queso
milk (*u*)	lait	leche
yogurt (*u*)	yaourt	yogurt
Fats and oils	*Matières grasses*	*Materias grasas*
butter	beurre	mantequilla
margarine	margarine	margarina
oil	huile	aceite
Cereals and cereal products	*Céréales et produits céréaliers*	*Cereales y productos de cereales*
barley (*u*)	orge	cebada
maize (*u*) (Am.E = corn)	maïs	maíz
oats (*c, pl*)	avoine	avena
wheat (*u*)	blé	trigo
flour (*u*)	farine	harina
bread (*u*)	pain	pan
(bread) roll (*c*)	petit pain	panecillo
rice (*u*)	riz	arroz
Condiments	*Condiments*	*Condimentos*
salt (*u*)	sel	sal
pepper (*u*)	poivre	pimienta
mustard (*u*)	moutarde	mostaza
vinegar (*u*)	vinaigre	vinagre

Italian	German	Greek
Latticini	*Milchprodukte*	Γαλακτοκομικά Προιόντα
panna	Sahne	κρέμα†
formaggio	Käse	τυρί
latte	Milch	γάλα
yogurt	Joghurt	γιαούρτι
Grassi ed olii	*Fett und Ölsorten*	Λίπη και έλαια
burro	Butter	βούτυρο
margarina	Margarine	μαγειρικό λίπος
olio	Öl	λαδι
Cereali e loro prodotti	*Getreidearten und Getreideprodukte*	Δημητριακά Προιόντα
orzo	Gerste	κριθάρι
granturco/mais	Mais	καλαμπόκι
avena	Hafer	βρώμη
grano	Weizen	σιτάρι
farina	Mehl	αλεύρι
pane	Brot	ψωμί
panino	Brötchen	ψωμάκι
riso	Reis	ρύζι
Condimenti	*Gewürze*	Καρυκεύματα
sale	Salz	αλάτι
pepe	Pfeffer	πιπέρι
mastarda/senape	Senf	μουστάρδα
aceto	Essig	ξύδι

English	**French**	**Spanish**
Herbs, etc.	*Fines herbes*	*Finas hierbas*
basil (*u*)	basilic	albahaca
bay leaves (*c, pl*)	laurier	laurel
chervil (*u*)	cerfeuil	perifollo
chilli (*u/c*) (-es) (Am.E. = chile/chiles)	piment	chile
chives (*c, pl*)	ciboulette	cebollino
garlic (*u*)	ail	ajo
mint (*u*)	menthe	menta, hierbabuena
parsley (*u*)	persil	perejil
rosemary (*u*)	romarin	romero
sage (*u*)	sauge	salvia
tarragon (*u*)	estragon	estragón
thyme (*u*)	thym	tomillo
Spices	*Epices*	*Especias*
cloves (*c, pl*)	clou de girofle	clavo
cinammon (*u*)	cannelle	canela
nutmeg (*u*)	muscade	nuez moscada
mace (*u*)	macis	macis
ginger (*u*)	gingembre	jengibre
saffron (*u*)	safran	azafrán
vanilla (*u*)	vanille	vainilla
Dessert ingredients	*Ingrédients pour desserts*	*Ingredientes para dulces*
honey (*u*)	miel	miel
jam (*u*)	confiture	mermelada, confitura
sugar (*u*)	sucre	azúcar
chocolate (*u*)	chocolat	chocolate

Italian	German	Greek
Erbe	*Kräuter*	Αρωματικά βότανα
basilico	Basilikum	βασιλικός
alloro	Lorbeer	φύλλο δάφνης
cerfoglio	Kerbel	φραγκομαιντανός
peperoncino	Chili	κόκκινη πιπεριά
erba cipollina	Schnittlauch	σκοινόπρασο
aglio	Knoblauch	σκόρδο
menta	Minze	δυόσμος
prezzemolo	Petersilie	μαιντανός
rosmarino	Rosmarin	δεντρολίβανο
salvia	Salbei	φασκόμηλο
dragoncello	Estragon	εστραγγόν
timo	Thymian	θυμάρι
Spezie	*Gewürze*	Μπαχαρικά
chiodo di garofano	Nelke	γαρύφαλα
cannella	Zimt	κανέλα
noce moscata	Muskatnuß	μοσχοκάρυδο
macis	Muskatblüte	μασίς
zenzero	Ingwer	πιπερόρριζα
zafferano	Safran	ζαφορά
vainiglia	Vanille	βανίλια
Ingredienti per dolci	*Nachtisch Zutaten*	Υλικά γλυκών
miele	Honig	μέλι
marmellata/confettura	Konfitüre	μαρμελάδα
zucchero	Zucker	ζάχαρη
cioccolato	Schokolade	σοκολάτα

English	French	Spanish
Sauces (u)	*Sauces*	*Salsas*
(*salad*) dressing (*u*)	assaisonnement (*salade*)	condimento (*de ensalada*)
gravy (*u*)	jus (*de viande*)	jugo de carne
mayonnaise (*u*)	mayonnaise	mayonesa

Miscellaneous

batter (*u*)	pâte à frire	batido
dough (*u*)	pâte	masa
dumpling (*c*)	gnocchi	noquis
ice cream (*u/c*)	glace	helado
jelly (*u/c*)	gelée	gelatina
meringue (*u/c*)	meringue	merengue
mousse (*u/c*)	mousse	mousse
omelet/omelette (*c*)	omelette	tortilla
pancake (*c*)	crêpe	crepa
pasta (*u*)	pâtes	pastas italianas
pastry (*u*)	pâte	masa, pasta
pie (*u/c*)	pâté	pastel
salad (*u/c*)	salade	ensalada
sausages (*u/c*)	saucisses	salchichas
soufflé (*u/c*)	soufflé	soufflé
stew (*u*)	sauté	estofado
tart (Am.E. = pie)	tarte	tarta

Adjectives describing food	*Adjectifs utilisés pour décrire des aliments*	*Adjetivos describiendo alimentos*
bitter	amer	amargo
cold	froid	frío
cooked (= not raw)	cuit	cocido
creamy	onctueux	untuoso
dried	sec	seco

Italian	German	Greek
Salse	*Saucen*	Συμπληρώματα
condimento per insalata	Salatdressing	λαδόξυδο
sugo di carne	Bratensauce	ζωμός, ψητού κρέατος
maionese	Mayonnaise	μαγιονέζα
pastella	Backteig	κουρκούτι
impasto	Teig	ζυμάρι
canederli	Klößchen	★★
gelato	Eis	παγωτό
gelatina	Gelee	ζελέ
meringa	Meringe	μαρέγκα
mousse	Mousse	μούς
frittata	Omelette	ομελέττα
crêpe	Pfannkuchen	τηγανίτα
pasta	Teigwaren	ζυμαρικά
impasto	Teig	ζύμη
tortino salato	Pastete	πίττα
insalata	Salat	σαλάτα
Salsicce	Würstchen	λουκάνικα
soufflé	Auflauf	σουφλέ
stufato	Ragout	βραστό
crostata	Torte	τάρτα
Aggettivi da adottare per i cibi	*Adjektive für Beschreibung von Lebensmitteln*	Επίθετα που περιγράφουν φαγητά
amaro	bitter	πικρό
freddo	kalt	κρύο
cotto	gekocht	μαγειρεμένο
cremoso	sahnig	κρεμαρισμένο
asciutto	getrocknet/Trocken-...	στεγνο, αποξηραμένο

English	**French**	**Spanish**

Adjectives describing food (cont.)

English	French	Spanish
fattening	grossissant	que engorda
fresh (= not dried/ tinned, etc.)	frais	fresco
heavy	lourd	pesado
hot (= not cold)	chaud	caliente
hot/spicy	piquant	picante
light (=not heavy/rich)	léger	ligero
pickled	mariné	marinado
raw	cru	crudo
rich	riche	indigesto
salty	salé	salado
smoked	fumé	ahumado
sour/tart	aigre	agrio
sweet	sucré	azucarado
tinned (Am.E = canned)	en conserve	en conserva

Verbs describing ways of cutting (past part. in brackets)	*Les différentes façons de découper*	*Distintos modos de cortar*
chop (chopped)	hacher (haché)	picar (picado)
cut (cut)	couper (coupé)	cortar (cortado)
fillet (filleted)	découper en filets (découpé...)	cortar en filetes (cortado...)
grate (grated)	râper (râpé)	rallar (rallado)
grind (ground)	moudre (moulu)	moler (molido)
mash (mashed)	faire en purée	hacerlo puré
mince (minced)	hacher (haché)	picar (picado)

Italian	German	Greek
ingrassante	macht dick	παχυντικό
fresco	frisch	φρέοκο
pesante	(liegt) schwer im Magen	βαρύ
caldo	warm	ζεστό
piccante	pikant	καυτερό (πιπεράτο, πικάντικο)
leggero	leicht	ελαφρό
sottaceto (i sottaceti)	mariniert	τουρσί
crudo	roh	ωμό
ricco	kalorienreich	θρεπτικό, βαρύ, παχύ
salato	gesalzen	αλμυρό
affumicato	geräuchert	καπνιστό
acido/agro	sauer	ξυνό
dolce	gezuckert	γλυκό
in scatola	Dosen-...	κονσέρβα

Verbi che descrivono i vari modi di tagliare	*Verschiedene Schneidearten*	Ρήματα που περιγράφουν τρόπους κοψίματος
spezzare (spezzato)	hacken (gehackt)	ψιλοκόβω (ψιλοκομένο)
tagliare (tagliato)	schneiden (gschnitten)	κόβω (κομμένο)
tagliare a filetti (tagliato...)	filieren (filetieren)	φιλετάρω (φιλαρισμένο)*
grattuggiare (grattuggiato)	reiben (gerieben)	ξύνω (ξυσμένο)
macinare (macinato)	mahlen (gemahlen)	αλέθω (αλεσμένο)
passare al setaccio (passato)	stampfen/pürieren	πολτοποιώ (πουρέ)
sminuzzare (sminuzzato)	hacken (gehackt)	κιμαδιάζω (κιμάς)

English	French	Spanish .

Verbs describing ways of cutting (cont.)

peel (peeled)	éplucher (épluché)	pelar (pelado)
slice (sliced)	couper en tranches	trinchar (trinchado)
,, ,,	,, ,, rondelles	rebanar (rebanado)

Verbs describing ways of cooking	*Les différentes cuissons*	*Distintos modos de cocción*
bake (baked)	cuire au four (cuit)	cocer al horno (cocido)
boil (boiled)	bouillir (bouilli)	hervir (hervido)
braise (braised)	étuver (étuvé)	estofar (estofado)
fry (fried)	frire (frit)	freír (frito)
grill (grilled) (Am.E = broil, broiled)	griller (grillé)	emparrillar (a la parrilla)
poach (poached)	pocher (poché)	hervir (hervido)
roast (roast)	rôtir (rôti)	asar (asado)
sauté (sautéd/sautéed)	faire sauter (sauté)	saltear (salteado)

Miscellaneous verbs describing preparation	*Les différentes préparations*	*Distintos modos de preparación*
beat (beaten), whip (whipped)	fouetter (fouetté)	batir (batido)
fill (filled)	remplir (rempli)	rellenar (rellenado)
flavour (flavoured)	assaisonner (assaisonné)	sazonar (sazonado)
garnish (garnished)	garnir (garni)	guarnecer (guarnecido)
mix (mixed)	mélanger (mélangé)	mezclar (mezclado)
stuff (stuffed)	farcir (farci)	rellenar (rellenado)

Italian	German	Greek
sbucciare (sbucciato)	schälen (geschält)	ξεφλουδίζω (ξεφλουδισμένα)
affetare (affettato)	in Scheibenschneiden (in Scheiben geschnitten)	κόβω σε φέτες (φέτες)

Modi di cottura	*Verschiedene Kocharten*	Ρήματα που περιγράφουν τρόπους μαγειρέματος
cuocere al forno (cotto...)	backen im Ofen (gebacken)	ψήνω
bollire (bollito)	kochen (gekochen)	βράζω
rosolare (rosolato)	dünsten (gedünstet)	★★
friggere (fritto)	fritieren (fritiert)	τηγανίζω
cuocere alla griglia cotto...)	grillen (gegrillt)	ψήνω στη σχάρα
affogare (affogato)	pochieren (pochiert)	ποσάρω
arrostire (arrostito)	braten (gebraten)	ψήνω
soffriggere (soffritto)	sautieren (sautiert)	σωτάρω

Preparazioni	*Verschiedene Vorbereitungsarten*	Διάφορα ρήματα που περιγράφουν
battere (battuto)	schlagen (geschlagen)	χτυπώ
riempire (riempito)	füllen (gefüllt)	γεμίζω
condire (condito)	würzen (gewurzt)	αρωματίζω
guarnire (guarnito)	garnieren (garniert)	γαρνίρω
mescolare (mescolato)	mischen (gemischt)	αναμιγνύω
farcire (farcito)	farcieren (gefüllt)	παραγεμίζω

Notes:* the word is rarely used ** only by description